Ayn Rand

Twayne's United States Authors Series

Warren French, Editor

University College of Swansea, Wales

TUSAS 501

"Man is a word that has no plural."
—Ayn Rand

Ayn Rand

By James T. Baker

Western Kentucky University

Twayne Publishers
A Division of G.K. Hall & Co. • Boston

Ayn Rand

James T. Baker

Copyright © 1987 by G.K. Hall & Co.
All Rights Reserved
Published by Twayne Publishers
A Division of G.K. Hall & Co.
70 Lincoln Street
Boston, Massachusetts 02111

Frontispiece photograph of Ayn Rand courtesy of
Leonard Peikoff, literary executor

Copyediting supervised by Lewis DeSimone
Book production by Marne B. Sultz
Book design by Barbara Anderson

Typeset in 11 pt. Garamond
by Modern Graphics, Inc., Weymouth, Massachusetts

Printed on permanent/durable acid-free paper
and bound in the United States of America

Library of Congress Cataloging in Publication Data

Baker, James Thomas.
  Ayn Rand.

  (Twayne's United States authors series ; TUSAS 501)
  Bibliography: p. 159
  Includes index.
  1. Rand, Ayn.   I. Title.   II. Series.
B945.R234B35   1987   191   86–29569
ISBN 0–8057–7497–1

To Barbara—
the Dagny Taggart of the Baker clan

Contents

About the Author

James T. Baker is professor of history and director of the University Honors Program at Western Kentucky University in Bowling Green. He received his B.A. in history from Baylor University in 1962 and his Ph.D. in humanities from Florida State University in 1968. While a graduate student he served as a college chaplain.

Dr. Baker is author of six books, among them biographical and critical studies of public figures as varied as Trappist poet Thomas Merton, California longshoreman and philosopher Eric Hoffer, and former president of the United States Jimmy Carter. He is also author of over a hundred articles that have appeared in nationally recognized journals.

In 1975 Baker studied at Harvard's Villa I Tatti near Florence, Italy. In 1977 he was Fulbright Professor of American History at Seoul National University in Korea. And in 1984 he was Fulbright Professor of American Studies at Tanjahn University in Taiwan. During the summer of 1986 he was director of the Kentucky Cooperative Center for Study in Britain at King's College of the University of London.

He is the father of two daughters, Virginia and Elizabeth, both students. One of his many goals is once again to appear, as he did at age nineteen, in Ayn Rand's *Night of January 16th*. His daughters have promised to cooperate with this endeavor.

Preface: The Woman

Ayn Rand was a name that appeared regularly on paperback books I noted but had no time to read as a college student. I would occasionally pick one up, attracted by the odd spelling of the first name, the provocative title, the lurid design; but I learned little more from my quick scans than the fact that she advocated radical economic self-interest and was the creator of a hero who destroyed the building he had designed when someone tampered with its facade.

This was of course a pitifully superficial summary of Ayn Rand's thought, as superficial as my hasty dismissal of her accomplishment and influence was cavalier. Mine were not far afield, however, from the analyses and dismissals the rest of the academic world gave her between 1940 and 1970. It was only in the post-Vietnam era, with neocapitalist emphases on ego enhancement and hero worship, that anyone outside her own tight circle of dedicated disciples recognized that she both reflected and helped restore to the American consciousness the recurring Myth of the Rugged Individualist.

Perhaps it is appropriate that in this volume she be rescued from the hands of both her admirers and her detractors, both of whom survive in abundance, that at long last she be given a fair and objective assessment, by someone who admittedly failed for a long time to recognize her achievement, who even today neither hates nor loves her, but who—I hope—sees her as she is.

Just as she once wrote that "man is a word that has no plural," so it can be said that Ayn Rand was a woman who had and still has no equal. She was one of a kind. Photographs show that she had Bette Davis eyes: large, intelligent, unafraid, yet surprisingly vulnerable. Recordings of her lectures and interviews reveal that she spoke with a Marlene Dietrich voice: deep, continental, richly stained with nicotine, seductive. Reproductions of her signature demonstrate a distinct style—plain and simple, straight up and down, heavy and decisive—reflecting the personality of a stern Russian conductor anxious to keep an undisciplined American orchestra of followers from deviation.

She was and is far greater than the sum of her distinctive personality, fiction, and philosophy. Only Tolstoy, in writing *War and Peace,* was as able to sustain an emotion for as long a time as Rand sustained her celebration of individualism in writing *The Fountainhead* or her disdain for altruism in writing *Atlas Shrugged* or her utter contempt for collectivism in writing her hundreds of articles on objectivism. It was a frightening energy, fueled by an unquestioning conviction, that forged the formidable force that was and is *Ayn Rand.*

It is my hope that this volume will clearly detail the life, the work, the themes and theories that earned Rand praise and condemnation, disciples and enemies. It is my further hope that it will identify and explain the enduring legacy she left to a world she so thoroughly explored, interpreted, reflected, and helped create.

James T. Baker

Western Kentucky University

Chronology

1905	Alissa Rosenbaum born 2 February in St. Petersburg, Russia.
1917	Eyewitness to the Russian Revolution.
1924	Graduates with major in history from University of Leningrad.
1926	Takes name Ayn Rand. Arrives in America; works until 1928 as movie extra and scriptwriter in Hollywood.
1929	Marries Frank O'Connor.
1929–1932	Works in R.K.O. wardrobe.
1931	Naturalized an American citizen.
1931–1933	Writes *We the Living,* "Red Pawn," and *Penthouse Legend.*
1932–1934	Screenwriter for Universal, Paramount, and M.G.M.
1934	*Penthouse Legend* produced in Hollywood as *Woman on Trial.*
1935	Moves to New York. *Night of January 16th* a Broadway success.
1936	*We the Living.*
1937	Works for Eli Jacques Kahn architectural firm. Begins writing *The Fountainhead.*
1938	*Anthem.*
1940	*The Unconquered* appears briefly on Broadway.
1941–1943	Scriptwriter for Paramount.
1943	*The Fountainhead.*
1944	Returns to California. Screenwriter for Hal Wallis Studios until 1949; writes filmscript for *The Fountainhead.*
1947	Testifies before House Un-American Activities Committee.

1949   Film version of *The Fountainhead.*

1950   Meets Nathaniel Branden.

1951   Moves permanently to New York City.

1957   *Atlas Shrugged.*

1961   *For the New Intellectual.*

1962–1965   Coedits and co-publishes *Objectivist Newsletter.*

1964   *The Virtue of Selfishness.*

1966–1971   Coedits and co-publishes *Objectivist.*

1966   *Capitalism: The Unknown Ideal.*

1967   *Introduction to Objectivist Epistemology.*

1968   Breaks with Nathaniel Branden.

1971–1976   Coedits and co-publishes *Ayn Rand Letter.*

1971   *The Romantic Manifesto* and *The New Left: The Anti-Industrial Revolution.*

1975   Undergoes surgery. Discontinues *Ayn Rand Letter.*

1979   Frank O'Connor dies.

1982   Ayn Rand dies 6 March in New York City. *Philosophy: Who Needs It?*

1984   *The Early Ayn Rand.*

Chapter One
The Life and Times of Ayn Rand

The woman who would become Ayn Rand was born in St. Petersburg, Russia on 2 February 1905, in the eleventh year of Nicholas II's reign. She died a world-famous American author in New York City on 6 March 1982, in the second year of Ronald Reagan's presidency. During the seventy-seven eventful years between these dates she wrote long-remembered plays, best-selling novels, and widely read philosophic essays. She founded her own school of social thought. Despite the ridicule of critics, both literary and philosophic, she attracted a following larger and more loyal than most writers know in their lifetimes. In death she continues to be a surprisingly, some would say frighteningly, strong force in American life and thought.

It may seem strange that a woman of no outstanding physical attraction, no charismatic public demeanor, no discernible lyrical beauty, certainly no gift for philosophic systematization would become so intellectually influential. But this small woman of extraordinary conviction, evergy, and passion, as soon as she arrived in America, recognized and went on to exploit and revive the most cherished of American myths. Future generations, like the last, will find her both attractive and repellent because her books will continue to revive, exploit, and perpetuate those myths.

Russia

Ayn Rand was born Alissa Rosenbaum, the oldest of three daughters of a Russian chemist. The family lived comfortably under the czar, and Alissa received a quality early education in private schools. Having learned to read and write at the age of six, two years before Russian children generally started school, she demonstrated strong academic skills, preferring mathematics to other, less demanding studies. But as time passed she found all her classes sufficiently

1

boring to start reading and writing short stories. One of the earliest
stories she would later remember writing was about a woman who
in time of crisis chose to save her husband before seeing to the safety
of her sick child.[1]

Throughout her life she remembered the first story, a serial, that
gripped her and helped mold her philosophy of life. It was called
"The Mysterious Valley,"[2] and it told the tale of an Englishman
named Cyrus who defeated an Indian rajah's attempt to overthrow
British rule. In this hero she saw the qualities of integrity and
courage she would spend her life describing in fiction and encour-
aging in philosophy. Cyrus, whose name she would give to Kira
Argounova in *We the Living* and to Karen Andre in *Night of January
16th,* would be her ideal man, a man in control of himself and of
his destiny, triumphant over the forces of chaos.[3]

Rand once said that her decision to be a writer, to dedicate her
life to re-creating Cyruses, came during a family vacation to London
in the summer of 1914, when she was nine years old. What experience or combination of experiences led to this decision is not
clear; but the decision was doubtless pressed into her memory by
the fact that the first shots of the Great War were fired that summer
and the Rosenbaums had difficulty making their way back to Russia
through hostile seas. As a schoolgirl back home, living through a
period of deep uncertainty, she began writing stories with all the
intensity the times demanded.

The war brought revolution, and in her thirteenth year Russia
went spinning from monarchy to democracy to communism. After
the Bolshevik victory her father's business was nationalized, and the
family's comfortable life abruptly ended. She would never forget or
forgive this reversal of fortune, and she would argue that the most
repugnant of Marxist doctrines was the secular altruism that called
for the sacrifice of the individual to the common good.

In 1918, as Russia surrendered to Germany and plunged into
civil war, her family hurried away to the Crimea. It was there that
Alissa discovered the novels of Victor Hugo, stories of heroic individuals fighting great adversity, and longed to write such stories
herself. She stretched reality by finding in the young Enjolras of
Les Misérables a freedom fighter against collectivism, particularly
considering Hugo's socialist convictions; but his unselfconscious
chivalry brought comfort and inspiration in an hour dark with terror
and shed new light on the path she had chosen.[4]

The Rosenbaums were nominally Jewish; but they did not keep

the traditions, and Alissa received no formal religious training. During the days in the Crimea she declared herself an atheist. She would hold to this personal conviction, with what some would call "religious" fervor, all her life. Even her admiration for America, the nation "under God," would not shake her atheism.

In long conversations with her father during this period of confusion and danger, she came to the conclusion that the idea of a God who dictates his will to man and demands that man humble himself in his presence, is degrading to man and antithetical to the image of man as hero.[5] Perhaps unconsciously adopting the thought of the hated but victorious Marxists, as other captives have adopted the faith of their captors, she concluded that man can never achieve greatness so long as he is burdened by a humiliating theism. Man must live not for the state or for others or for God, she decided, but only for himself.

In 1921, when she was sixteen, she returned with her family to the city of her birth, now called Petrograd, eventually to be Leningrad; and there she entered the university. She was advised by family, friends, and political authorities to study engineering, a field that offered someone of her capabilities advancement in the emerging industrial state; but in typical individualistic style she rejected all such advice. Mathematics and logic, she said, were only means to the end of learning to order one's mind, to the development of an integrated vision of the world, not ways to earn a living. She chose instead the impractical study of history. She wrote little fiction at university. These were years to watch, listen, and store up impressions and information. The only record of creative endeavor during this time was an outline she made for a play that was never written but which would serve as inspiration for what would much later be the novel *Anthem*. It would be the story of a man fighting a heroic battle to rediscover manhood in a totalitarian society.

Rand later recalled that at university she read and was converted to the "rationalist" philosophy of Aristotle, while at the same time reading and being repelled by the "mysticism" of Plato. She retained this conviction and choice throughout her life. It was also at university that she read Nietzsche and rejected his contention that man's primary drive is to gain power over his fellowman. Man's primary drive, she argued, is productivity. She also read Dostoyevski and was saddened that such a gifted writer would be burdened by an unneccessary and debilitating mysticism.[6]

Literature gained from her years at university the novels *Anthem* and *We the Living,* both of which she wrote in America a full fifteen years after graduation. Of the two, *We the Living* is the more obvious reflection of her university experience. Its heroine, Kira, is a student of engineering who dreams of building skyscrapers like the ones she sees in photographs of New York City, who refuses to conform to the Soviet system, and who dies trying to escape the country on foot in the snow. She lives amid the poverty, hunger, and disease of the classless society, in the ruins of a family reduced to penury. Like Kira, Alissa lived through such adverse conditions; and like Kira she seems to have fallen in love with a young student who challenged the system, but who unlike Kira's young man was sent into Siberian exile. Like Kira, she found comfort in the few operettas and Hollywood films permitted to be shown in Petrograd; and like Kira, she was saved from despair by their themes of heroic battles against the enemies of happiness.

Upon graduation in 1924, when she was nineteen, Alissa took a job as a guide in one of Petrograd's historical museums, as did Kira, and remained a servant of the Soviet state for over a year. But late in 1925 came a letter from her Lipski and Portnoy relatives in Chicago inviting her to come to the United States for a visit. She considered the invitation a pardon from prison. She applied for a passport, still not daring hope that the government would comply, and to her amazement it was granted. She knew when she left home that she would never return; and as she made her way west she changed her name to Ayn. Ayn was the name of a Finnish writer she admired. Rand, which became her name soon after she arrived in America, was taken from the Remington-Rand on her typewriter.

Ayn Rand doubtless sounded more "American" to her than Alissa Rosenbaum; and Ayn—which rhymed with *mine*—assured that she would be noticed and remembered. The new name represented to her a new life, and this was what she wanted above all things. She later recalled leaving her native land, and the name associated with it, with relief and "complete loathing" for its system.[7] She never saw her parents or her older sister again. They died in Russia. She saw her younger sister fifty years later in the United States, but the reunion was not pleasant.

Hollywood

Early in 1926 Rand was on her way to the West, and in February she celebrated her twenty-first birthday in Berlin. It was snowing when she first set eyes on the New York City skyline, and she had fifty dollars in her pocket. She made her way to Chicago, dreaming of going on to Hollywood. That summer, as she worked to improve her English, she wrote four scenarios she hoped to sell to a movie studio. At the end of the summer, armed only with manuscripts and a letter of recommendation to the Cecil B. DeMille Studio from one of DeMille's Chicago distributors, she set out for paradise.

In a postscript to *Atlas Shrugged,* she would write about her earliest days in America: "No one helped me, nor did I think at any time that it was anyone's duty to help me." This declaration of independence neatly suited her myth of the self-made individualist; but it is not true. It did take immense courage and fortitude for a young woman alone to make such a journey in distance, time, and culture. She took chances, she worked hard, and she deserved the success that eventually came to her. But without the support of her family, both in Russia and in America, without the help of that film distributor in Chicago, without the kindnesses of nameless, faceless people along the way, she would never have achieved her goals.

She was also lucky. After moving into a room at the Hollywood Studio Club, she set out for the DeMille Studio and on the first day found a job. Mostly apocryphal is the story she later told friends of how DeMille himself drove past her as she waited outside the gate, stopped to offer his help, was impressed that she had come all the way from Russia to work for him, gave her a ride inside, and put her to work as an extra on *The King of Kings.*[8] Whatever the real story, she did become an extra for crowd scenes in the 1926 version of the life of Jesus. It was an auspicious beginning.

Although she later recalled how superficial she found Hollywood in the 1920s, Rand worked for DeMille until his studio closed and remained in Hollywood for nine years. After another nine years away, she returned for seven more. She spent a large part of her life trying to write for the screen. Hollywood was never good to her, but it taught her about writing and about human nature.

At first she earned her living as an extra while spending her free hours writing scenarios and synopses that she hopefully submitted to DeMille's office; all, however, were rejected. The power brokers, perhaps put off by her somewhat obscure English, considered her work unrealistic, "improbable," not "human" enough for popular audiences. If the short stories she wrote at the same time are any indication of the themes and style of her scenarios, then she was indeed out of Hollywood's mainstream. The language of the extant pieces is tedious, the characters blatantly Olympian, the ambiences otherworldly. They are full of the action, adventure, heroism, and romantic love that made her later work—with its more realistic language and settings—so successful. Perhaps what she lacked in those early days was the philosophic passion and conviction that would make the later work so powerful and thus so attractive or repellent to readers. The early stories are too easy on contemporary society, not yet outraged enough to be characteristic of novelist Ayn Rand.

While her offerings were rejected by the film lords, her persistence finally paid off. DeMille made her a junior screenwriter only a few weeks after her arrival, and she earned twenty-five dollars a week until the studio closed in 1928. It was during these months that she read 0. Henry; and some of her own stories of this period imitate his style and endings. She desperately wanted to be a successful American author. She would later recall being terribly impressed at this time by a novel called *Calumet "K"* by Merwin and Webster, a story about a young architect who overcame great obstacles to build a grain elevator in the Midwest.[9] In a preface to a later edition of that book she praised its hero's "ingenuity in solving unexpected problems and smashing through sudden obstacles, his self-confident resourcefulness, his inexhaustible energy, his dedication." Howard Roark and *The Fountainhead* were already gestating.

Perhaps as significant for her future as her writing apprenticeship during these early days was Rand's romance with Frank O'Connor. He was to take the place of the boy lost to Siberia and remain her companion the rest of her life. Charles Francis O'Connor, born in 1898 in Lorain, Ohio, the youngest son of a steel mill foreman, was of Irish descent, as several of Rand's heroes would be. A Roman Catholic who after meeting Rand obligingly recalled that since childhood he had doubted his faith, he was tall and fair, the opposite of the small, dark Rand, a man who looked like the Cyrus of her childhood romance. She first saw him on "Jerusalem" street when they were both extras in *The King of Kings*.

O'Connor, whom she married in 1929, was the perfect mate for Ayn Rand. As a boy he had wanted to paint and after school had gone to New York to try his hand at acting. He had followed the studios as they transferred to California. He was never more than a bit player in pictures; but he was, according to those who knew him best, a handsome, passive, nonintellectual fellow, liked by all, alcoholic, a person who accepted his lot in life without bitterness. [10] Despite his fair complexion and resolute dedication to labor, he was nothing like the heroes Rand said he inspired. [11]

He would faithfully, placidly follow Rand to New York, back to Hollywood, back again to New York, teaching himself new trades, adjusting to her career, tolerating with humor her odd passions, making suggestions without pressing. Rand would identify him as her model for Howard Roark in *The Fountainhead,* would credit him with giving her the theme for *Atlas Shrugged,* and would dedicate both novels to him, although he would have to share the latter with a younger man in her life. They would be married for fifty years, until his death in 1979, and he would provide the security that permitted her to write and lecture and develop her philosophy. Psychologists might take great pleasure pondering the way this tame man met the needs of this passionate woman.

Early in 1928 the DeMille Studio closed; and for a time both Rand and O'Connor were out of work. Rand spent the next year and a half at odd jobs, often waiting tables, always in places where O'Connor would not see her doing menial labor. [12] Despite or perhaps because of their economic plight, they decided in the spring of 1929 to merge their meager assets. They were married, made a trip to Mexico, and Ayn Rand O'Connor returned to the United States as the wife of an American citizen. Almost immediately she applied for citizenship herself, and in 1931 she was naturalized. [13]

Soon after their marriage, in the summer of 1929, Rand landed a job with the wardrobe department of R.K.O. Studios. She stayed there until 1932, working her way up from filing clerk to head of the department. [14] By her own account she hated this job and the three years she gave to it; and her frustration shows in a short story from this period called "Her Second Career," the account of a woman who first surrenders her inner integrity and then abandons her moral values. Yet Rand continued to work at wardrobe, and with apparent success, in order to pay the bills while continuing to write during her spare time.

Along with the short stories she began writing the novel that was eventually published in 1936 as *We the Living.* In 1932 she sold a story and its screenplay, "Red Pawn," to Universal Pictures. It was about a woman who schemed to become the mistress of a prison commandant in order to be near her prisoner husband. [15] The idea of a woman who gives herself to one man to save another, the *Tosca* theme, would appear again in *We the Living, The Fountainhead,* and *Atlas Shrugged.* Rand's fantasy was of a woman surrounded by strong men competing for her love. "Red Pawn" at first disturbed and confused studio readers, as had her earlier work. She was told that life was simply not like this; and her answer was, "It should be." Eventually enough people agreed, the story sold, and Rand's literary career was launched.

Then came a frustration greater than the early rejections. Universal, having paid her $1,500, traded the story to Paramount for a story that had cost $20,000, and Paramount decided not to make it into a film.[16] It was in fact never produced, and except for the $1,500 all Rand realized from the sale was a chance to move out of R.K.O.'s wardrobe and into a brief career as a screenwriter for Universal, Paramount, and M.G.M. From 1932 through 1934 she moved between these studios, leaving behind her a litter of scripts she considered beneath her talent and dignity, all the while spending every spare moment writing a novel and a play.

The novel was *We the Living.* Begun in 1931 and completed in 1933, it was not published until 1936, when Rand was living in New York City, following a success on Broadway with *Night of January 16th.* The language in this novel was more "American" than in her previous attempts, the story more cogent and consistent, and the characters more believable, being based on real people she had known during her days at the university. Still, it was initially considered too "intellectual" for a popular audience and rejected for publication. Perhaps this meant that a female writer had no business being intellectual. Perhaps it meant that the story was anti-Soviet. Many Americans, with their country embroiled in a depression with no end in sight, had begun to think of the Soviet system as a noble experiment in economic equality; and a voice so strident in its denunciations of the collectivist state was unwelcome. Rand made no apologies for either the style or the content of her story. She in fact said that its primary purpose was to awaken the American public to the evils of the Soviet system as she had known it. Thus the novel waited for a push from another Rand story, this one produced on the stage and an immediate success.

At the time she was finishing the manuscript for *We the Living,* in 1932–33, Rand wrote what would be her first literary success, a play that would make her name famous and give her a platform from which to preach her philosophy, but which would also cause her more grief than all her rejections together. It was a play about a woman named Karen Andre who is accused of murdering her millionaire lover. It featured the interesting twist of a jury chosen directly from the evening's audience and had two endings, depending on whether the jury found Andre innocent or guilty that night. Since the murdered man had been thrown from a Manhattan penthouse apartment, Rand called it *Penthouse Legend.*

Rand could have sold the play to A. H. Woods, a successful New York producer, who wanted to take it to Broadway; but she was afraid that by this transaction she might lose control of the work. Instead she signed a contract with E. E. Clive to do it at the Hollywood Playhouse. Clive produced the play much as Rand had written it, except that the name was changed to the more provocative *Woman on Trial,* and Rand was happy with the results. It opened in October 1934 and had a successful run. Critics praised it for what Rand considered all the wrong reasons: the flair, the colorful characters, the gimmicky ending. To her it was supposed to be more than a mere murder mystery, more than an assortment of bizarre characters, more than clever tricks. She saw it as an expression of her philosophy of life, with heroes and villains whose high or low moralities grew out of epistemological attitudes toward life, and she was about the only person who saw it that way. She reluctantly accepted the laurels, promising herself that she would be more explicit in future renderings.

New York

With the Hollywood success under her belt, Rand felt confident to take on Broadway and signed with A. H. Woods under terms even better than he had offered earlier. In the spring of 1935 she and Frank O'Connor drove across depression America, west to east, not knowing what they would find in New York: they found what Rand later called a year of pure hell. She indeed lost control of her play. Its name was changed again, this time to *Night of January 16th,* and she had to fight constantly to retain as much as possible of its original integrity. At one point, owing to the feud between author and producer, its opening was delayed indefinitely. The O'Connors meanwhile lived on the edge of poverty.

At last, in the autumn of 1935, what Rand called the mangled corpse of her play opened. One of opening night's jurors was prize fighter Jack Dempsey, another Edward J. Reilly, who had unsuccessfully defended Bruno Hauptman in the Lindbergh baby kidnapping case. *Night of January 16th* was an immediate and prolonged success, receiving mostly favorable reviews—again for all the wrong reasons—by the nation's most critical press and running for seven months on Broadway. Rand came to feel that she was herself the woman on trial. In 1936 she sued Woods for royalties he was paying another writer for rewriting portions of the script. A badly edited and censored version of the manuscript was illegally disseminated and produced. It was only in 1968 that the play was published as she had originally written it. Her only bow to popular memory then was to let it be called *Night of January 16th* instead of *Penthouse Legend.* That concession was withdrawn when in 1973 it was revived in a New York production.

So 1935 was, despite the play's success, not a good year. Rand was frustrated by the battle over the play; she could not sell *We the Living;* and New York was inhospitable. The universe was not a benevolent place. In December she began making notes for a story about an architect like the grain elevator builder in *Calumet "K."* Although the play brought money and *We the Living* was published the next year, neither of these events brought her much joy; and the new book's heroine, Dominique Francon, would be a dark pessimist, "myself in a bad mood," Rand would later describe her.

We the Living, published in March 1936 by Macmillan, received mixed reviews. Critics found it "good reading, bad pleading," which meant that she had permitted ideology to intrude upon her fiction. Some saw in her indictment of the Soviet system the bias of a former member of the privileged class, a loser, reduced to verbal broadsides against the winners. Macmillan was reticent to spend much money advertising a first novel; and when early sales were not particularly good the type was destroyed. Sales began to pick up after a year, due to word-of-mouth recommendations, but no effort was made to reissue it, and only the initial 3,000 copies were sold. In 1959, after the success of *Atlas Shrugged,* the long neglected *We the Living* was released by Random House; and in 1960 New American Library brought it out in a paperback edition. To date it has sold over a half million copies and sells consistently well.

The public's reception of *We the Living* proved a preview of the public response to all of Rand's fiction. Publishers and critics were cool to her work; initial sales were slow; and each book grew more popular as years passed. Rand was always an outsider in the literary world, a writer whose appeal was to audiences, not to the establishment. She must have longed for the acceptance of fellow writers and critics, but she never admitted that she was anything but pleased with a struggle for acceptance that never came. It made her all the more the individualist she had tended to be from the start. It made her Ayn Rand.

During the latter part of 1936 and much of 1937 Rand read everything she could find on the subject of architecture. She took a job as an unpaid typist for the Eli Jacques Kahn architectural firm in order to learn the business side of the profession.[17] She was preparing herself to write a great novel, which would be as much a philosophic treatise as an entertainment, about an architect who would also be a hero.

The Fountainhead, written over the next six years, features four men. Architect Howard Roark is its protagonist: an Irish-American from a Midwestern steel-mill town, a man of great ego and independent judgment, the master of his own fate. Peter Keating, another architect, early rich and famous, later a complete and utter failure, is Roark's negative mirror image: a man with little true sense of self-worth who looks to others for moral leadership and loses control of his own fate. Gail Wynand, newspaper publisher and the most tragic of the four, is a Howard Roark who fails by yielding to the will of society, loses control of his fate, and ends up on the slagheap of history. Ellsworth Toohey, a writer, an intellectual, a man whose ego was long ago turned toward the Nietzschean drive for power, serves as Roark's antagonist and the novel's chief villain. Floating among these men is Dominique Francon, Rand herself in a bad mood, who eventually sleeps with three of the men and draws sustenance from their enlarging and/or shrinking egos.

Early in her writing Rand determined that this would be Howard Roark's story. She was tired of stories about human failure. In her previous fiction she had permitted her characters to be dragged down by social forces and inner weaknesses; but while Roark faces tremendous adversity, he ultimately triumphs. *The Fountainhead* was to be no Faulknerian slough of despond, nor was it to be a Shakespearean tragedy. It was to be no slice of ordinary life, but an extraordinary story about an extraordinary man who in the end wins an extraordinary victory.

During the summer of 1937 Rand left the Kahn firm and went to Connecticut, where Frank O'Connor was playing with a theatrical stock company. There she wrote the novel that had started out as an outline for a play during her university days in Russia. She called it *Anthem*. It was a brief—hardly more than 20,000 words—dystopia that described in what would later be called Orwellian style the plight of a man living under a collectivist system. She found no American publisher for it, despite its "happy" ending, but in 1938 it was published in Britain. It was published in this country by Pamphleteers in 1946 and in hardcover by Caxton in 1953, following the success of *The Fountainhead*. New American Library eventually offered it at a popular paperback price, and it was made into a comic book for children.

In 1939 Rand adapted her "underground best-selling" novel *We the Living* for the stage; and the next year it opened on Broadway, under the title *The Unconquered*. Critics panned it as farfetched and anti-Soviet, and it soon closed. Also in 1939 she wrote but found no producer for her third and last play, "Think Twice." Without the gimmickry of *Night of January 16th,* the work had no real attraction for the popular theater. Small wonder that she gave up on the stage and turned to fiction. Small wonder too that as she wrote Dominique Francon's story she was in a bad mood.

As America moved toward war in 1940, Rand found herself attracted to politics. It was the year for a presidential election. She had long disliked Franklin Roosevelt's social programs; and she saw in his Republican opponent a creditable alternative to the "leftist" drift of the Democrats. Despite her precarious financial status, she spent nearly three months of 1940 campaigning for Wendell Willkie. She was convinced that his victory would save the free enterprise system. Her efforts were wasted as Willkie went down to defeat, the incumbent president's third victim in three contests; and Rand was inconsolable, devastated not just by the defeat but by Willkie's "betrayal" of his troops. She blamed his "me-too-ism" for losing the race and called him a general who had led his soldiers to slaughter. With her naive vision of American history and politics and of the American psyche, she failed to understand Roosevelt's grip on the American imagination and concluded that if Willkie had only been a more faithful champion of capitalism the Republicans would have won the election.[18]

Republicans in the 1950s and 1960s would express Rand's frustration when they began to call for "a choice, not an echo"; but in the 1940s they rallied around the wartime president and lost Rand's respect, particularly as Roosevelt allied the country with the Soviet Union. By the time Republicans came around to Rand's viewpoint, she had concluded that neither party could be trusted to introduce the revolution needed to save the nation. While she continued to favor Republicans over Democrats, she found little to cheer in any party except Barry Goldwater in 1964 and to a lesser degree Gerald Ford in 1976. She was particularly incensed by Ronald Reagan, who posed as a conservative but favored a mixed economy and laws limiting personal liberties.

Late in 1940, financially desperate, Rand returned to pictures. She went to work for Paramount's New York office as a script reader and kept at this tedious work, taking breaks to write, through 1943 when *The Fountainhead* was published. She had completed only one-third of this giant novel when in 1941 she began trying to sell it. Again came the predictable rejections; and it is difficult to say whether Howard Roark would ever have seen the light of day had Bobbs-Merrill editor Archibald Ogden not acted as Rand's benefactor.

Ogden threatened to leave the firm if his superiors refused the unfinished manuscript. Rand later offered some verbal gymnastics to prove that this was not an act of self-sacrifice, that she was not the recipient of another person's altruism, as she argued that Ogden was simply acting out of self-interest as he fought to be the man who discovered a great piece of literature. Whatever the case, by December 1941 he had wrestled a contract from the jaws of rejection, and Rand was told she had to bring in a completed manuscript by January 1943. Taking leaves of absence from Paramount, she worked most of 1942 on the book, met her deadline, and saw the massive work published in May 1943.

The Fountainhead was to be a resounding and perpetual success, though not an immediate one. Dedicated to Frank O'Connor, with his painting "Man Also Rises" adorning its cover, it received moderately positive reviews. Among the few "intelligent" reviews—by Rand's standards—was one by Lorine Pruette in the *New York Times*. Pruette caught the point Rand wanted to make about individualism's superiority to collectivism. Pruette also understood that this novel of ideas (she was surprised to find a woman writing such a book) would require readers to rethink many of the basic assumptions of the day.[19]

Although initial sales were slow, by November 1943 they had risen to 18,000; and by the end of the year Rand sold the screen rights, with herself designated to do the screenplay, to Warner Brothers for $50,000. The night she learned of the sale she rewarded herself with a sixty-five-cent instead of her usual forty-five-cent dinner at the local restaurant where she customarily dined; but soon she cast her reticence to the wind and bought herself a mink coat. She was relearning affluent ways.

Hollywood—Again

Having driven from California to New York through depression America in 1935, the O'Connors returned west in 1944—this time traveling through wartime America by rail, and enjoying the luxury of a Pullman. The trip may have solidified an idea for a new novel, one still nebulous that Rand said Frank O'Connor suggested to her in the form of a question some weeks earlier: What if all the intelligent individualists in America decided one day no longer to support a mixed capitalist-socialist system they no longer trusted? What if they all went on strike? Rand would in time tie this question and its answer to a woman who ran a railroad, surround her with four Howard Roarks, and after thirteen years produce *Atlas Shrugged*. With Rand now living in luxury and basking in fame, that woman would be in a better mood than Dominique Francon of *The Fountainhead*.

Meanwhile a screenplay of *The Fountainhead* had to be written. This took six months. Rand vowed when it was finished that she would never again convert one of her novels into a script, and she kept her promise, although when she died she was said to be preparing a television play for a production of *Atlas Shrugged*. She found the work on *The Fountainhead* tedious and frustrating. After it was finished she learned that production would be delayed until the end of the war; and in fact it waited four years to be made and five to reach the public.

Although Rand was now solvent, she took a job in late 1944 as a screenwriter for Hall Wallis, a former Warner Brothers producer who was opening his own studio. She remained with Wallis until

1949, when she was financially secure enough to devote herself full-time to writing. In the meantime her contract with Wallis called for her to work half of each year, with six months remaining to do her own writing. Among her film "successes" of this period were *Love Letters* and *You Came Along,* and by the time she left Wallis she was earning $35,000 a year. But the sales of *The Fountainhead* and her desire to complete the story about intellectuals who go out on strike led to her declaration of independence.[20]

In 1945 she was invited to architect Frank Lloyd Wright's famous home Taliesen East. Many people believe Wright was the model for Howard Roark, and he indicated in the invitation that he had read and heartily approved *The Fountainhead.* The meeting was a great success, and Wright later designed a house for Rand to build in New York, one he considered proper for her personality, a three-storied affair with her study at the top.[21] Unfortunately, it was never built, Rand preferring upon her return to the city to live in a Manhattan apartment rather than a house upriver.

The home that Rand and O'Connor bought near Tarzana in the San Fernando Vally, their home until 1951, was designed by Richard Neutra and had belonged to Marlene Dietrich; and it was as appropriate to the Rand mystique as a house could be. It was set on thirteen acres of land covered with fruit trees, and along with tending to the grounds and trees O'Connor occupied himself with growing orchids for commercial sale and raising peacocks for pleasure. *House and Garden* featured this house in a 1949 article, describing in some detail its aluminum-covered steel walls, its black marble floors, and its moat. Frank Lloyd Wright would have approved the setting.[22]

By 1945 *The Fountainhead* had sold 10,000 copies; and another company offered Warner Brothers $450,000 for the screen rights. Warner refused the offer and made promises to complete the film as soon as possible. Rand turned her attention to other matters and in 1946 composed the first lines of what would become *Atlas Shrugged.*

At this time she also involved herself in the postwar attempt to sniff and snuff out left-leaning Hollywood writers and actors. America was, in light of Russian perfidy, reassessing its relationship with the Soviet Union. The depression-age admiration for and the war-time desire to cooperate with the Russians took a radical swing toward suspicion and hostility. Russian sympathizers were accused and punished. Rand volunteered to be an accuser.

In her *Screen Guide for Americans,* written for the Motion Picture

Alliance for the Preservation of American Ideals, she claimed that there was an appalling amount of communist propaganda in Hollywood films of the time. Never mind that during the war Washington had urged Hollywood to buttress the allied cause by praising Russia; now the House Committee on Un-American Activities gave Rand the chance to testify against those people who had scoffed at her anti-Soviet fiction; and in 1947 she gladly appeared before HUAC to condemn the "Hollywood Ten." At long last the public heard the message those communists had kept her from delivering for so long.[23]

By 1948 *The Fountainhead* had topped the half million mark in sales; and in 1949 the film version was released in an atmosphere that seemed perfect for its success. Warner Brothers and Bobbs-Merrill cooperated to guarantee that the film would be as big a hit as the book. It was billed as the faithful dramatization of the novel so many people loved.[24] The result was a jump in sales for the book, with 50,000 copies sold in six months at three dollars a copy, with a New American Library paperback edition pushing total sales past the two million mark by 1952. Yet the lavish advertising campaign, the drawing power of Gary Cooper as Howard Roark and the young Patricia Neal as Dominique Francon, and Rand's gift for translating the story to film all failed to make the picture a hit.

In 1950, as Rand licked her wounds over this failure and began turning out the first chapters of another novel, she met a man who would have a great influence on her life and thought. His name was Nathaniel Branden, and he would be a fan, then a disciple, and finally her organizer, director, and official spokesman. His wife, Barbara, now says he was from 1955 to 1958 also her lover.

Born Nathan Blumenthal in Canada, Branden was a student of psychology at U.C.L.A. Early in 1950 he wrote Rand a fan letter, telling her that he had read *The Fountainhead* many times and considered it a masterpiece. Rand invited him to her home for a visit, immediately recognized in him a kindred spirit, and took him under her maternal (he was one day to say paternal) wing. Soon they were sharing all-night tutorials, expressing a common faith in the heroic nature of man, and celebrating their common liberation from Judaic theism. He was permitted to read *Atlas Shurgged* as it was written; and in 1957 she dedicated it to both Frank O'Connor, whose character inspired the story's heroes, and Branden, an "ideal reader" and her "intellectual heir." So he would be until 1968.

Branden brought his girlfriend Barbara Weidman, a philosophy student and the future Mrs. Branden, to meet Rand; and Barbara became the second of her personal disciples. Rand served as Barbara's matron of honor and Frank O'Connor as Branden's best man when the young couple married in New York City some months later. The Brandens, husband and wife, were to play key roles in the rise and fall of public philosopher Ayn Rand.

New York—Again

It was almost certainly Branden's decision to study for a doctorate at New York University in 1951 that led Rand to conclude she had lived long enough in sunny California and to move back to New York herself. The O'Connors did not leave the city again; and it was in a small apartment in the East Thirties, while Frank worked as a florist, that Rand finished writing *Atlas Shrugged.*

The mammoth book was completed in 1957, after nine years of writing. The soon-to-be-famous "radio address of John Galt," which would be quoted as scripture by Rand and her followers for the next quarter century, took two years to complete.[25] The 35,000 words and seventy pages of its final form were a condensation of the earliest outpouring of Rand's anticollectivist, anti-altruistic emotions. Rand supporters and critics alike agree that this is the essence of her philosophy of life, politics, and economics. When Random House publisher Bennett Cerf recommended that it be abbreviated, Rand asked him if he would also recommend cutting the Bible.

Atlas Shrugged, published by Random House on 10 October 1957, was widely reviewed, for the most part negatively. Yet the book sold amazingly well, from the start this time, with sales of 125,000 the first year. Rand obviously had a following. To date it has sold, in hardback and paper, over two million copies, despite being labeled wordy, didactic, repetitious, and as one reviewer said, "a masochist's lollipop."[26] It was her last novel, her last work of fiction; for by 1958 she had become a philosopher.

From the publication of *Atlas Shrugged* until her death in 1982, Rand dedicated herself exclusively to writing philosophic essays. She went out of her apartment only to lecture and hold seminars at the Branden Institute. Her social life was limited to "tutorials" with her inner circle. Her life was philosophy: to correct errors in modern thought, to outline a plan for America's future. Frank O'Connor, during this time, returned to his first love, art, studied at the New York Art Students League, became a respectable painter, but still remained a faithful husband to the philosophic genius he had married.

Rand came to call her chosen disciples, the inner circle of the larger following, "the children" and "the Class of '43" after the publication date of *The Fountainhead.* They included Nathaniel and Barbara Branden, Barbara's cousin Leonard Peikoff (one day to replace Branden as intellectual heir-apparent), Branden's sister Elayne Kalberman (who became circulation manager for Rand's variously named journals), and Alan Greenspan (one day to be Gerald Ford's chairman of the President's Council of Economic Advisers). These people listened to Rand's pronouncements, confirmed her convictions, and served as field generals in her campaign to enlighten America with the philosophy of Objectivism.

By 1958 Nathaniel Branden had assembled a series of twenty lectures on Rand's philosophy. They proved so popular and there was such a demand for a formal structure to promote her ideas that Branden closed his private psychotherapy practice and opened the Nathaniel Branden Institute. Rand reluctantly gave the enterprise her blessing and agreed to participate in sessions Branden planned to hold. The Institute was first housed in the Sheraton-Atlantic Hotel at 34th and Broadway and later in the Empire State Building. Aspiring Objectivists paid tuition to hear Branden lecture, Rand answer questions, and eventually to be inducted into the Senior Collective, made up of those who had successfully completed the course twice, read and agreed with all of Rand's books, and promised to live purely by the dictates of reason.[27] The Objectivist movement, inspired by Rand and directed by Branden, was on track.

Slowly but surely Rand earned respect as someone who could do more than write novels. In 1958 she raised eyebrows with comments made to CBS reporter Mike Wallace in an interview. In 1960, just into the decade that would see her become a philosopher, she was a visiting lecturer at Columbia, Princeton, and Yale. *Time* covered the latter address, which was part of the Yale Challenge Series, and reported some of her more provocative pronouncements: Kant is the father of all modern philosophic errors; altruism is America's besetting weakness; capitalism is the foundation of all political freedoms; and "The cross is the symbol of torture; I prefer the dollar sign, the symbol of free trade, therefore of the free mind."[28] This last statement, made earlier to Wallace, had been widely quoted in the press and always drew a strong reaction.

In 1961 she published her first philosophic treatise, a book called *For the New Intellectual*. Only the first section, the title essay, some sixty-five pages, was previously unpublished. The rest were selections from *We the Living, Anthem, The Fountainhead,* and *Atlas Shrugged,* arranged to illustrate the new essay. This book, with its subtitle "The Philosophy of Ayn Rand," announced to the world that she was to be taken seriously as a philosopher. That year, in addition to lectures at Wisconsin, Johns Hopkins, and Syracuse, she presented a formal address at the Ford Hall Forum in Boston, where she gave an annual lecture until the year she died.

In March 1961 *Newsweek* did a story on her called "Born Eccentric." The anonymous reporter described a typical evening with Branden and Rand at the Nathaniel Branden Institute. All the "new intellectuals" listened patiently as Branden droned on for three hours, discoursing on "Ayn Rand and Ethics," "Ayn Rand and Aesthetics," "Ayn Rand and Love," preparing them for the moment Rand would appear to answer questions. The reporter found her an impressive figure, despite her stocky build, because her dark, penetrating eyes could "wilt a cactus." Her thick Russian voice intimidated doubters and scoffers, while her "dollar sign" gold broach impressed the faithful. He concluded that "there hasn't been a she-messiah since Aimee McPherson who can so hypnotize a live audience."[29] As to one of her arguments, that America is too altruistic, he advised her to correct this misapprehension by riding on any New York subway. Rand demanded more of this reporter than a straight factual story.

In November 1961 John Kobler, in a *Saturday Evening Post* story called "Curious Cult of Ayn Rand," described his own reaction as he listened to that voice as richly Russian as blintzes on sour cream. He found her almost completely devoid of grace, with a personality as compelling as a sledgehammer, slow to smile, on guard against laughter, intolerant of humor. She had recently demanded a public apology from the Syracuse University newspaper for describing her philosophy as a form of Nazism, and had refused to give a lecture there until the university issued a disclaimer. Kobler called her the free enterprise system's Joan of Arc, with a Yankee dollar her Cross of Lorraine.[30] It is obvious that Rand was making quite an impression in this first year of the Kennedy presidency.

The year 1962 found her delivering addresses at Columbia, Harvard, and MIT. It also saw the birth of a journal designed to spread Rand's thought. The *Objectivist Newsletter* was a four-page monthly that lasted for forty-eight issues, from January 1962 through December 1965. With Rand and Branden as coeditors and copublishers, it featured articles, essays, and lectures by Rand, articles by Branden, and occasional pieces by members of the "Class of '43"— Peikoff, Greenspan, Robert Hessen, and Edith Efron. There were reviews of books Rand favored and a calendar of events for faithful Objectivists to attend. The subscription list grew steadily as students were graduated from the Institute; and early in 1966 the *Newsletter* was transformed into a magazine called the *Objectivist*.

In 1962 the Brandens' book *Who Is Ayn Rand?* was published by Random House (as had been *Atlas Shrugged*), its title derived from the question, "Who is John Galt?" Its brisk sales demonstrated how intriguing the public found the new philosopher. A paperback edition boosted sales further, and it helped spread Rand's story to an ever-widening audience. Barbara Branden's biography is much better written than Nathaniel's obtuse analysis of Rand's ideas, but overall the book is helpful if uncritical.

In 1963 Rand received a measure of academic respectability when she was granted a Doctor of Humane Letters degree from Lewis and Clark College in Portland, Oregon. In 1964 she set a pattern for all her later books by publishing *The Virtue of Selfishness,* composed of lectures and essays from the *Objectivist Newsletter* and issued in paperback by New American Library. This was the first of many such collections of Rand essays published by this company.

Also in 1964 she began a series of radio broadcasts called "Ayn Rand on Campus" from Columbia University and a series called "Commentary" that aired on a New York City F.M. station. Perhaps more significant, because it proved that she had become a pop culture star, was the March 1964 *Playboy* interview with Alvin Toffler. Toffler described the woman he met several times over several weeks, this "fountainhead of objectivism," as an "intense, angry young woman of 58" who was *sui generis,* "indubitably, irrevocably, intransigently individual."[31] She chain-smoked her way through the sessions, using her blue-and-silver cigarette holder, a gift from admirers, engraved with her initials, the names of three heroes from *Atlas Shrugged,* and diminutive dollar signs. The interview proved that she had opinions on every subject, from world peace to human sexuality, and that she was not afraid to speak her mind.

In 1964 Rand supported Barry Goldwater for president, the first public endorsement she had given a candidate since 1940, and again she was disappointed in the election results. She saw Goldwater as the kind of "Atlas" who would return America to capitalism. She was particularly distressed that the public thought of the detestable Lyndon Johnson as a political John Wayne, when it was obvious to her that he was nothing more than a socialist like Wesley Mouch. The election only confirmed her conviction that America was headed down the road to ruin.

In 1966 the *Newsletter* became the *Objectivist,* a sixteen-page monthly, that served as Objectivism's mouthpiece for sixty-nine issues, through years of great upheaval for the movement, until it returned to a simpler form as the *Ayn Rand Letter* in September 1971. The new format permitted Rand and Branden to publish longer articles than before, some of them with complicated themes, and at its height in late 1967 it claimed a subscription list of 21,000. It was also in 1966 that Rand published a second volume of essays, collected from the journals, provocatively entitled *Capitalism: The Unknown Ideal.* Most of the pieces were Rand's but there were two by Nathaniel Branden, three by Alan Greenspan, and one by Robert Hessen, all of the inner circle.

This book was followed, in 1967, by Rand's *Introduction to Objectivist Epistemology.* For years Rand had threatened to write a systematic philosophy of her thought; and she described this book as a first chapter, an overture, to that work. No further chapters appeared, however, and Objectivism remained unsystematized. Also in 1967 there appared a *Life* article called "The Cult of Angry Ayn Rand," by Dora Jane Hamblin. The author, after calling attention to the 3,500 students and 25,000 graduates of the Nathaniel Branden Institute, described Rand's followers as the quietest and least hairy of all the young radicals of the 1960s. They were button-down revolutionaries, young men and women in their twenties and thirties who were neatly dressed, often wealthy by inheritance or with promising careers, who enjoyed hearing Rand say that they deserved all the good things that had come their way and that those who would tax them were evil.[32] The Objectivist movement, Hamblin mused, was an elaborate house of cards held up by Rand's personality. Her followers were as much cartoon characters as the figures in her fiction. They existed because she said they did.

Objectivism

In 1968, at what proved to be the height of the Objectivist movement, as if following a universal law of such movements, Rand's house of cards came tumbling down and had to be reassembled by new leadership. For some years she had grown more intolerant, opinionated, autocratic—strange qualities for the leader of a movement dedicated to individualism. Bennett Cerf, her publisher and an observer, blamed her attitude on sycophantic followers who gained power in the movement by stroking her ego to the point of rupture. Nathaniel Branden, who did the most stroking, blamed it on years of intellectual isolation. Whatever the cause, Rand's increasing suspicion of deviation in her ranks, her conviction that the only true interpretation of reality was her own, and her determination to keep her movement pure led to quarrels, purges, and finally a schism.

The most dramatic quarrel—and cause of the schism—was with her second-in-command, Nathaniel Branden. Rand and Branden had by 1968 collected an intimidating host of true believers. Jerome Tuccille, one disenchanted member of the clan, later recalled that they were all jutjawed, humorless, competitive types who tended to ape Rand by wearing capes and dollar sign pins and smoking cigarettes (nonsmoking was "anti-life") from silver holders. They were all expected to agree with every word Rand or Branden said; and they were all required to follow the *Atlas* creed, which they recited at initiation: "I swear—by my life and my love of it—that I will never live for another man, nor ask another man to live for mine."[33] Branden was both the creator and victim of this society.

This conformist organization marching under the banner of freedom and individualism was in time, as if by natural law, to come to grief, blown apart by an explosion at the top. In the May 1968 edition of the *Objectivist,* strangely delayed until September, there appeared an article by Rand entitled "To Whom It May Concern." In it she repudiated Nathaniel and Barbara and dissociated them from herself and the movement. What they had written prior to this time was orthodox Objectivism, but from this point on they were to speak only for themselves. "I hereby withdraw my endorsement of them and their future works and activities. I repudiate both of them, totally and permanently, as spokesman for me or for Objectivism." In the 1970 editions of both *The Virtue of Selfishness* and *Capitalism: The Unknown Ideal,* she retained Branden's articles but added a footnote to the preface: "Nathaniel Branden is no longer associated with me, with my philosophy or with *The Objectivist.*"

Shocked fans and followers had to wonder what was happening. Rand's article on the rupture, her first and last word on the subject, accused Branden of deception, exploitation, and moral transgressions. What did all this mean? Some believed it had to do with the fact that the Brandens were about to divorce. Nathaniel had supposedly been engaged in a love affair with one "Patricia Wynand," whose name sounds suspiciously like something out of *The Fountainhead.* But this explanation must be considered an inadequate solution to the riddle, despite Rand's somewhat old-fashioned attitudes toward marriage, attitudes not reflected in her novels, because it does not explain why she also dissociated herself from an innocent Barbara and not just from a guilty Nathaniel.

Rand's own statement said, without elaboration, that the Brandens (apparently both of them) had tried to profit from her name— a strange accusation from one who had long deified capitalism's profit motive. What did this mean? In what way did the Brandens try to get rich off Ayn Rand's name? In what way did they try to do something that she had not known about for years? An article in the March edition of the *Objectivist,* just two months before the ax began to fall, provides a partial answer. It announced that the Nathaniel Branden Institute was about to create a new organization called the Foundation for the New Intellectual, a federally registered and thus tax-exempted foundation for the perpetuation of Objectivism.[34] Branden and Peikoff were to be its trustees. Had Rand not been consulted? Did the sixty-three-year-old writer feel that she was being ignored, exploited? Was she offended that her heir-apparent was willing to make peace with, take a bribe from the hated collectivist government? Did she fear that dealing with federal subsidies might compromise her movement? Possibly. Yet she did not insist that the foundation be dissolved, and it continues to this day. Furthermore, she did not purge Leonard Peikoff, Branden's partner, and made him the movement's new leader and her own new intellectual heir-apparent. There was more.

The rest of the story is told in Barbara Branden's new book, *The*

Passion of Ayn Rand. Barbara says that Rand virtually forced her and Nathaniel to marry and then took Nathaniel from her. She says that from 1955 on Rand and Branden spent one afternoon and night a week alone together, while Rand insisted that neither her own marriage to Frank O'Connor nor Nathaniel's to Barbara be ended. The relationship was sexual. Barbara's reaction was to grow cold, Frank's to descend into alcoholism.

In 1965 Barbara and Nathaniel separated and Nathaniel took one Patricia Gullison as his lover. Although his relationship with Rand was now less intensely sexual, when in 1968 he refused to sleep with her any longer, she exploded. She publicly condemned him, calling him a morally corrupt, irrational monster, and expelling him from her movement. His only rebuttal was a letter entitled "In Answer to Ayn Rand," which he mailed to *Objectivist* subscribers, denying any wrong-doing and hinting darkly that he was purged for rejecting an old woman's misguided romantic overtures.[35]

Whatever the truth, there did occur what disillusioned disciple Sid Greenberg has labeled an "Objectischism." Branden was out, Peikoff was in—as coeditor and copublisher of the *Objectivist,* as lecturer on Objectivism, and as executor of Ayn Rand's estate, her intellectual heir-apparent. All those who wanted to remain with Rand would be required to take a loyalty oath. Branden closed his institute and moved to California, where he remarried and established his Biocentric Institute. He eventually distributed a tape on his experience with Rand, the rewards and dangers of working with her, his debt to her and hers to him. In a 1978 dinner speech he admitted this debt once more and defended the theories they had jointly developed; but he also accused her of irrational behavior and hinted that this woman of such great intellectual gifts was psychologically unbalanced.[36] He repudiated the book *Who Is Ayn Rand* and wrote several more of his own, mostly based on articles that first appeared in the *Objectivist Newsletter* and the *Objectivist,* but rewritten with new twists to make them seem original. He remained basically an Objectivist, albeit in fresh clothing.

Meanwhile the movement back in New York was in trouble. The *Objectivist,* only recently moved to more spacious quarters, was forced to return to its modest accommodations. The institute that had so successfully recruited and trained Objectivists was closed. Peikoff lacked Branden's dynamism, though he was a better speaker and writer than Branden, and there seemed a paucity of leadership.

Branden loyalists and those disenchanted by the rumors surrounding
the schism were slipping away. The true believers and Rand loyalists
took the oath of fealty and gamely carried on. Those caught somewhere in the middle, attracted more by the libertarian than the
authoritarian nature of Objectivism, drifted away into politics, some
Republican, some Libertarian. Others merely drifted. The movement, its embittered leader forced to manage without Branden,
slowly declined.

Rand was still in a bad mood the next year. She sued Avon Books
for using her name on the cover of a paperback book without her
permission. It seems that in a review of Eugene Vale's *Chaos Below
Heaven* a *San Francisco Chronicle* writer had likened Vale's style and
concerns to those of Ayn Rand; and on the cover of the paperback
edition Avon had quoted the review. Rand's suit accused Avon of
invading her privacy and of using her name "for purposes of trade"
without her permission. She did not flinch when opponents pointed
out that this "radical for capitalism" was calling for restraint of
trade. Her argument was that Avon was socialistic for not paying
her for the use of her product, her name. A lower court found for
her, but a month later an appellate court reversed the decision and
declared Avon innocent of breaking any New York law.[37] The result
only confirmed Rand's opinion of the present condition of American
law.

In 1971, as the movement continued to decline, Rand announced
that the *Objectivist* would be put to rest and be replaced by a typed
and mimeographed, three-to-four-page fortnightly publication called
simply the *Ayn Rand Letter.* It was to be, as its name indicates, a
longish letter from Rand herself to her followers, providing them
with an Objectivist interpretation of national and world affairs. The
Letter was to run for eighty-one issues, seventy-seven of them written
entirely by Rand, with Leonard Peikoff permitted on four occasions
to add to the copy, from October 1971 through January-February
1976, appearing less and less regularly toward the end of the period
and finally staggering to its death early in 1976.

Also in 1971 there appeared two more collections of previously
published essays, *The Romantic Manifesto* and *The New Left: The Anti-
Industrial Revolution.* As in the past, New American Library did the
honors. It is interesting to read in her preface to *The New Left* that
Rand was inspired to collect this particular group of essays by a fan
letter from a graduate student in sociology at Northern Illinois

University, referred to only as G.M.B., who begged her to bring out a book to instruct the rising neoconservative American college student. Even at sixty-six Rand could be stirred by a letter from an inquisitive young college man, as she had been twenty years before by one from the young U.C.L.A. man Nathaniel Branden. The neoconservative movement referred to here was soon to be a reality, soon to dominate American college campuses, and Ayn Rand was to be credited with leading this dramatic shift in student opinion and attitude.

Both in 1968 and in 1972 Rand reluctantly supported Richard Nixon for president, but only because she found Hubert Humphrey and George McGovern advocates of the welfare state she so despised. In 1972 she wrote a *Saturday Review* article accusing McGovern of being the greatest threat in history to American values.[38] She admitted that she could not be sure what Nixon would do but that she was certain McGovern would bring the nation to ruin. Nixon was not, however, her hero. She attacked him during his first term for his wage and price controls and for visiting Communist China; and she showed him no pity when during the two years following his landslide reelection in 1972 he fell into disrepute and was fored to resign the presidency.

The Final Curtain

The next years were for Ayn Rand a time of declining health and diminishing productivity. In 1973 *Night of January 16th* was revived, under its original title, *Penthouse Legend,* and using its original script, at the McAlpin Rooftop Theater in Manhattan. Reviews were negative, and no one wanted to prolong the agony. In 1974 there came a surprise message from her younger sister Nora, whom Rand had not seen since 1926. This woman had attended an American cultural exhibit in Moscow and recognized the featured writer "Ayn Rand" as her sister. It took weeks to verify the kinship, but when this was done she was permitted to come to the states for a visit. Almost upon her arrival the sisters began to quarrel. Rand's anticommunist tirades were bitter medicine for someone raised under Soviet tutelege to swallow. Rand begged her to stay in the land of freedom, but she returned to Russia.[39] The affair seemed to contribute to Rand's declining state of mind and body.

But it was also in 1974 that Rand traveled to Washington to see her old pupil and disciple Alan Greenspan sworn in as Gerald Ford's chairman of the President's Council of Economic Advisers. *Time* magazine reported that both Rand and Greenspan took pains to deny that she would advise Ford's adviser while he held office, but they agreed that free trade and minimal governmental restraints made for a healthy economy. Rand seemed delighted to be once again in the limelight. She chain-smoked Tareytons from the familiar blue and silver holder, took time to chide Alexander Solzhenitsyn for his faith in Russian Orthodox Christianity, and approved of Ford as president for "marvelous casting in appearance alone."[40]

In 1975 Rand's physical condition deteriorated, and in May her *Letter* was cut back to a monthly publication. That summer came surgery. There is disagreement as to its nature and effect on Rand's future. Mimi Gladstein has written that a lung was removed.[41] Leonard Peikoff says that a coin-sized lesion, found to be benign, was removed from a lung. Barbara Branden writes that one lobe, adjacent lymph nodes, and a rib were removed. She agrees with Gladstein that Rand had cancer. She also says that while Rand gave up smoking she refused to admit in print that she had cancer or to modify her position that Objectivists should smoke.[42] Rand pronounced her surgery a success and promised that she would soon be back to normal; but November brought word that the *Letter* would be discontinued and subscriptions refunded. The last edition, claiming that Objectivism was now the philosophic wave of the future, appeared early in 1976, three years before Margaret Thatcher became prime minister of Great Britain and five before Ronald Reagan became president of the United States. Rand would live to see both events.

She continued to deliver her annual lectures at the Ford Hall Forum in Boston; and she took some interest in politics, preferring Ford over Reagan (whose views on abortion she despised) in the Republican primaries of 1976; but time was running out for her. In November 1979, a few months after they celebrated their fiftieth anniversary, Frank O'Connor died. In 1981 she roused herself to deliver a speech before the National Commission for Monetary Reform in New Orleans and to meet and be reconciled with Barbara Branden. Later that year she was said to be making some progress on a television script for *Atlas Shrugged*. It was reportedly one-fourth complete when on 6 March 1982, in her seventy-eighth year, she died in her East 34th Street Manhattan apartment. Only a professional nurse was with her when she died. Her funeral, conducted by the Campbell Funeral Home on Madison Avenue, was a secular service on Tuesday, 9 March. She was buried next to Frank O'Connor at the Kensico Cemetary in Valhalla, New York.[43]

Rand had always said that she preferred making her own way. She consistently belittled any help she might have received from people she met. She confessed her love for Frank O'Connor and the inspiration he had been to her; but she insisted that even their love was essentially selfish, that it was mutual self-interest, that primarily they were beneficial to each other. She said that motherhood should be entirely voluntary, if chosen a full-time job, and that she was unwilling to sacrifice herself to a child. Her family would be her disciples. She was a hard woman who chose to live a hard life, and she will be a hard act to follow.

Leonard Peikoff has continued the tradition, giving lectures on Objectivism, writing more books, editing heretofore unpublished articles for new Rand editions. In 1982 he completed and published a collection that Rand had been compiling at the time of her death, and named it for one of its essays, *Philosophy: Who Needs It?* In 1984, after moving to southern California, he published a collection of unpublished fiction under the title *The Early Ayn Rand.* Several more volumes of unpublished and/or uncollected manuscripts await his attention; and he apparently has no plan to release Rand's private papers to the Library of Congress, as was her wish, until such matters are completed. In February 1985 he opened a new Ayn Rand Institute, complete with a newsletter, with himself as chairman of the board.

Peikoff has abandoned the city Rand loved so dearly for the state she hated; but he continues to run the movement from sunny California. The flight of so many Objectivists, both the faithful and the disillusioned, to that part of the nation has prompted one observer, a somewhat uncharitable critic who will remain anonymous, to comment that someone must have raised the United States at Boston and let all the loose nuts slide down to Orange County. Be that as it may, Objectivism still flourishes, if with diminished vitality, in soil seemingly even more hospitable to it than the steel buildings and concrete streets of Rand's New York.

Chapter Two

Ayn Rand as Creative Writer

Most people familiar with Ayn Rand know her primarily as the author of *Night of January 16th, The Fountainhead,* and/or *Atlas Shrugged.* They may be vaguely aware of her strong social and political opinions, but few remember her as a philosopher, and fewer still know her philosophic essays. Her fame, for better or worse, rests on her fiction.

This is no real cause for regret, for while her philosophy has its strengths and her fiction its weaknesses, the fiction is far and away her more lasting achievement. She wrote at least one stage play and two novels that deserve to be counted among the landmarks of twentieth-century American literature. Though they are all imperfect, primarily because they are so conspicuously and unremittingly ideological, they have met the psychological and aesthetic needs of multitudes of readers, perhaps owing to the very energy of their ideological biases. They may never be included among the "American Classics," but they have passed one major test of classicism: they will live on.

The Early Fiction

Although Alissa Rosenbaum decided to be a writer when she was nine years old and wrote a number of short stories and made outlines for novels and plays before leaving Russia, Rand was forced upon her arrival in the States in 1926, at age twenty-one, to start over—with a new language in a new land with a new culture. Yet she did not become a "Russian émigré" writer; nor did she abandon, despite frustrations, her dream of being famous. She started right in, perhaps haltingly, to write fiction in English, and she kept at it until she was successful.

Rand's executor, Leonard Peikoff, has collected in *The Early Ayn Rand* her unpublished first work, from the period between her arrival in this country to the time she was writing *Penthouse Legend* and *We the Living* six years later. These stories provide an interesting window through which to view her development. They show how quickly she mastered a new tongue. They show how rapidly her fluid images and principles crystallized into characters and action. They show her becoming an "American" writer, yet remaining essentially a unique individual in her adopted country.

The first of these stories, written in 1926, is called "The Husband I Bought." The English is remarkably good for someone so recently "off the boat," and it dispels some of the mystery of how Rand so quickly landed a job in Hollywood. The story's protagonist, Irene Wilmer, is an early Kira Argounova of *We the Living.* Her husband, Henry Stafford, is an early version of Leo from the same novel, or perhaps even an early Howard Roark of *The Fountainhead.* The story was written while Rand was doing scenarios for silent pictures; she signed it Allen Raynor, perhaps still uncertain of her identity.

Henry Stafford loses his wealth and Irene marries him, pays off his debts, and restores him to polite society, thus "buying" herself a husband. But she loves—actually worships—the man so much that when he falls in love with another woman, she pretends to have an affair with another man so that Henry will think she has been unfaithful and grant her a divorce. In the end he marries the other woman and lives happily ever after while Irene lives her life alone, satisfied that she has done the right thing, kneeling before his photograph in tribute to this ideal man.

There are hints here of the later Ayn Rand. Already we see the strong, intelligent woman worshipping a man who brings out the best in her. Already there is the strong element of masochism. Already there is the individualism that never looks back, never feels remorse. Leonard Peikoff suggests that Rand's attitude toward romantic love may have been formed as much by losing an early love to Siberian exile as by reading nineteenth-century fiction;[1] and if so we may be dealing with a writer whose romantic tendencies will always be dependent on a twist of irony.

Yet in Rand's second story another, contradictory tendency is already raising its head, one that will eventually lead in a more positive direction—Rand's love for the happy ending, the kind that grace (some say disgrace) her mature novels. "Good Copy," written in 1927, was completed while Rand worked for DeMille; and it is much like the synopses she was writing at the time: pure romantic fantasy, with daring heroes, loving heroines, slapdash action, and happy endings. There is virtually no philosophic content. Its English is better than that of "The Husband I Bought."

A reporter named Laury McGee is stuck in a small-time job with a small newspaper without prospects when he comes up with a great idea: he will kidnap a pretty young heiress named Jinx Winford, hold her hostage while he scoops all the competition with inside information on the abduction, and make himself famous. Naturally things go wrong. While he is making hay with his stories, a real kidnapper takes Jinx from him, threatens her life, and forces McGee to go to the police with the whole story. The quick-witted Jinx, however, escapes the bad guy and tells the world that the first kidnapping was a ruse to cover her elopement with the man she loves, McGee. They live happily ever after.

For Rand in those days happy endings came easily, for life was good. But soon there came rejection and with it a return to the dark Russian psyche of earlier times. She would long, while writing the wrenching *We the Living, The Fountainhead,* and *Atlas Shrugged,* to do stories with lighthearted themes. She even had a name, Faustin Donnegal, for the slaphappy Irish boy who would star in her farces (*E,* 35). But she seemed never to free herself from the pessimism of the late 1920s and early 1930s; and despite what she called victorious, "happy" endings, her later fiction was called comic opera only by uncharitable critics.

The early years saw a great deal of experimentation. Rand read and liked the stories of O. Henry and tried to match his light manner and surprise endings. A story called "Escort," written in 1929, the year she married, is a good example. It was signed O. O. Lyons for Oscar and Oswald, a pair of stuffed lions O'Connor had given her (*E,* 71). In the story the young husband Larry Dean keeps from his wife, Sue, the fact that he pays the rent by working as a professional escort, showing rich ladies around town while Sue stays home each night. Sue is so lonely that she uses her meager savings to hire an escort for one night of dancing. Both feel guilty about what they are doing and will doubtless feel more guilty shortly after the story ends; for Sue calls the service where Larry works, and Larry is told to pick up a "Mrs. Dean" at his own address.

There is little here of the later, darker Ayn Rand, except perhaps the thrill of trying to buy a man. There is a great deal here of the Ayn Rand who kept a stiff upper lip when she could find only

menial jobs and was married to an actor out of work who might be
earning his keep in ways she did not know.

So far Rand's stories, despite strong hints of Russian pessimism,
were more or less upbeat, with strong women who knew what they
wanted and got it. A fourth story, "Her Second Career," also written
in 1929 but after Rand had started working for R.K.O.'s wardrobe
department, features a woman who loses control of her life. Also
signed O. O. Lyons, this is the story of one Claire Nash, a starlet
in a Hollywood that is superficial, trite, and vain. Claire is so sure
that her success is due to talent—as perhaps Rand believed about
her own early success at DeMille—that she makes a bet she can
fake a European holiday, take a new name, and make it big a second
time on merit alone.

She soon discovers the hopeless plight of an unknown extra,
working for greedy, mindless, dictatorial directors (with German
accents), herded around back lots with other human livestock, growing ever more aware of life's injustices. At last she books herself
home from her fictitious vacation and prepares to meet her public
on the day the plane she is supposed to be flying arrives in Los
Angeles. The plane crashes and she is presumed dead. Her advisers
tell her that a grieving public would hate her if they learned of her
deception. She must indeed assume a new identity and start all over.
The story ends with her playing a bit part in a film that features a
girl she once discouraged from continuing a career in films. Critics
are cool to the "amateur" who had once been a star.

About all that can be said for "Her Second Career" is that it
shows Rand in that "bad mood" she would retain most of the rest
of her writing career. She was in fact entering a new phase in her
American life, one in which she would find more rejection than
acceptance, and she was not amused. She felt unappreciated, used,
angry. Yet out of her anger she would create three heroines, Joan
Volkontez of "Red Pawn," Kira Argounova of We the Living, and
Karen Andre of Penthouse Legend, the best female characters of all
her fiction, all three courageous, all three lovers of strong men, all
three assaulted but unconquered by injustice. Adversity was for
Rand the mother of invention.

She was writing Penthouse Legend and We the Living when in 1932
she sold the story "Red Pawn" to Universal Studios. Although it
was never produced, it enabled her to leave R.K.O. wardrobe. The
synopsis demonstrates Rand's flair for the dramatic. It also dem-

onstrates her antisocialist bias, which in the 1930s worked against the story's production and retarded the success of *We the Living.* The setting of "Red Pawn" was unfamiliar to Hollywood producers, its characters improbable, its ideology unacceptable. Its energy and plot sold it.

"Red Pawn" is the story of a strong young woman—in early versions a Russian countess, in later ones an American married to a Russian activist—who sets out to free her husband from prison by any means necessary. Frances Volkontez assumes a new identity, calling herself Joan, and volunteers to be mistress to a prison island's commandant, Comrade Kareyev. This will be a familiar theme in Rand's later fiction, what some call her *Tosca* theme, that of a woman who gives herself sexually to one man to save another.

Joan becomes Kareyev's mistress and arranges an escape—for a moment—for her dying husband. In the process she learns to love Kareyev, who is a good man serving an evil system, and he helps them escape. When they are caught she is told that her husband, "the convict," must return to the island to be executed, while she and the commandant are to go on to trial for conspiracy. She identifies the commandant as the convict, the commandant does not dispute her, and she takes her husband away to trial, knowing he will at least die on the mainland, as the commandant returns to the island to be executed. The commandant goes to his death with his head held high for the first time in years.

As in *We the Living,* Rand's true souls in "Red Pawn" do not survive the cruel Soviet system; but again they end their lives with dignity. With these two stories Rand seems to have found her message. *Penthouse Legend* still leaves a woman's fate in the hands of an unpredictable jury, and *The Fountainhead* and *Atlas Shrugged* shift the focus of attention to male characters as well as to North America; but by 1932 Rand had committed herself to the tale of the individual against the collectivist state, in *The Fountainhead* a state run by men without taste, in *Atlas Shrugged* a state run by men without reason.

Night of January 16th

Frustration with "Red Pawn," a script that sold but was not produced, led to further frustration with *Penthouse Legend*, a script that sold and was produced. Rand claimed that she had merely set out to write a courtroom drama about a woman on trial for pushing her wealthy boss-lover from a Manhattan penthouse, a play in which each night's jury would be chosen from the audience. Once she began writing, however, she decided to do this and much more; yet the woman on trial for killing her lover and the "gimmick" of selecting the jury from the audience were to be what most people enjoyed and remembered about the play. Even those who found the story simplistic, the characters cardboard, and the dialogue childish admitted and still admit that the play, with its female lead and its "gimmick," is worth an evening.

The story was inspired by public reaction to the suicide of Swedish "match king" Ivar Kreugar on 12 March 1932, followed almost immediately by the collapse of his financial empire. He had lent money to several European governments in exchange for match monopolies, the governments had reneged on their payments, and his company had gone bankrupt. Rand noted the "spree of gloating malice" at his death and the failure of his corporation, how he was one day called a genius and the next denounced as a criminal, and she concluded that it was not his dishonesty but his ambition and success that mediocre people despised. The play would be her vehicle for telling what she considered the truth about the life of such a man and the public's judgment of him.[2]

She called the play *Penthouse Legend* and would prefer that title the rest of her life. It opened in Hollywood in the fall of 1934 under the direction of veteran character actor E. E. Clive, with the title *Woman on Trial,* Clive's choice. While the production was too "naturalistic" for Rand, she gloried in its success; and after a year battling New York producer A. H. Woods, what Rand called its "mangled corpse" opened on Broadway in September 1935. It was directed by John Hayden and appeared under Woods's title, *Night of January 16th.* Despite its success, Rand took no pleasure in it.

Reviews gave most of the credit for success to producer Woods and to leading lady Doris Nolan. *News-Week* did not even mention Rand, referring instead to Woods's more than three hundred previous productions and to the fact that eighty of them over a thirty-year period had run longer than a year. The article commended him for discovering Miss Nolan but did not note the discovery of Ayn Rand.[3] *Commonweal* did call the play "well constructed, well enough written, admirably directed . . . and excellently acted," particularly by Doris Nolan; but it referred to the author, only once, as "Mr. Rand."[4]

Time got Rand's name and sex right but spent most of its space on Woods's previous successes, particularly his similar 1927 hit *The Trial of Mary Dugan*. *Night of January 16th*, it did admit, went *Mary Dugan* one trick better by selecting its jury from the audience.[5] But *Theatre Arts* dismissed the play as no more than a parlor game: "It is fun in a parlor with some bright wits about. It seems pretty foolish in a theatre."[6] No one caught Rand's deeper meanings, the clash of philosophies, the praise of heroic behavior, the ultimate victory of individualism; but this did not surprise her at all. No one foresaw great things for the author, and this undoubtedly surprised, angered, and frustrated her. The play ran for six months, not a Woods record but a successful run; and Karen Andre was found not guilty of the murder sixty percent of the time. This too was frustrating for Rand because she often said it should have been obvious to everyone that the woman was innocent.

The rest of the play's history, until 1968 when Rand's official edition was published, was "pure hell." In 1936 she sued Woods for paying another writer to make changes in the script. An unauthorized "amateur" version, which mangled the script even more than Woods had done, became popular with little theater groups around the country and an embarrassment to the author. A film version was, according to Rand, "cheap, trashy," and a further source of embarrassment. The whole experience taught her never to trust anyone with her work again. From this time she would guard her manuscripts, defending them against editing as though they were Holy Writ.

In 1960 the Nathaniel Branden Institute decided to do a public reading of the play, and Rand returned to her original manuscripts to provide the players with an authentic script. In 1968 that script was published by New American Library as the definitive text; the only bow to popular taste Rand made was to retain the title *Night of January 16th*. Otherwise it was all hers again, completely and forever, and she welcomed it home like a long lost child. At last she could be proud of it, and in a long preface she explained what the play was originally intended to say and do. A Manhattan revival, with her blessing, was held at the McAlpin Rooftop Theater beginning 22 February 1973, this time under the title *Penthouse Legend*. It had only a brief run, with few favorable reviews, and Rand put it to rest.

What surprises many readers of the play—and despite the magic of the lighted stage even some who see it performed—is its inaccurate portrayal of an American courtroom trial. One has to wonder if Rand had ever really spent time in court. At several points in the action the judge could and should declare a mistrial. Toward the end of act 3 there certainly should be a recess until two bodies are identified. The case against Karen Andre, which probably should never have come to trial, has been lost long before the jury is asked to decide her fate. In short, it is one of the most contrived courtroom dramas in the history of the theater. But of course the play was never intended to portray real life, certainly not the life of a courtroom, and audiences across the years have found the revelations of shady business deals and illicit love affairs so much fun that they have forgiven the play's shortcomings.

In act 1 the prosecution argues that on the night of January 16th, just before the Faulkner financial empire fell, Bjorn Faulkner's secretary-mistress pushed him from the Faulkner Building's penthouse to his death on a Manhattan street below. The doctor who examined the body is unable to say if the man were dead before he fell or had been previously wounded or even how long he had been dead when he was examined. The night watchman explains that Faulkner and Andre lived in the penthouse together until his marriage the previous October and that Andre then lived there alone. At 10:30 P.M. the night of January 16th, Faulkner, Andre, and two men entered the building, one of the men drunk, and went upstairs. Later the drunk man, now somewhat sobered, came down and left on foot, followed by a car; and later still the second man left. After an hour there were screams, Andre appeared in the lobby with her dress torn, and when the night watchman followed her outside he found the body on the street.

A private investigator hired by Faulkner's wife to watch him verifies that Faulkner, Andre, and the two unidentified men entered the building, the two men later left, and then he swears he saw Andre push Faulkner off the balcony. The defense is able to weaken this testimony by making the private eye admit he had tossed a few drinks while he waited in another building. A police investigator tells of finding Faulkner's "suicide note" in the penthouse and of taking Andre's immediate testimony that Faulkner had made his intentions known to her, struggled with her as she tried to stop him, and jumped to his death. The housekeeper makes no effort to hide her contempt for Andre, describing how Faulkner wasted money on her and how she saw her kissing another man the day Faulkner married Nancy Lee Whitfield. The man she was kissing, by the way, was one of those who came up to the penthouse January 16th.

Faulkner's wife, Nancy Lee, daughter of financier John Graham Whitfield, describes how she met her husband the previous August, married him in October, and loved him very much, as he did her. She admits that when she met him he had overextended himself financially and was on the verge of bankruptcy and that her father had bailed him out; but she contends that he married her for love and that he gladly dismissed Karen Andre after he proposed to her. She says that she hired a private investigator to watch Faulkner because a gangster named "Guts" Regan had threatened his life, not because she ever suspected his fidelity. The act ends with insults hurled between Nancy Lee and Karen Andre.

Act 2 brings to the stand financier Whitfield, Nancy Lee's father. He admits lending his new son-in-law $25 million and argues that Faulkner could have survived his crisis had he not died. He also admits irreconcilable differences between himself and Faulkner over money and social responsibility, what Rand would call in the 1968 preface to the published edition their "sense of life." As Whitfield puts it: "I believe in one's duty above all; Bjorn believed in nothing beyond his own pleasure." Rand would say that the play's primary purpose was to make a clear distinction between these two types of men.

At this point the prosecution rests, without making much of a case, and the defense begins. A handwriting expert explains that it is possible but not probable that Karen Andre forged the suicide note. Faulkner's male secretary, Siegurd Jungquist, demonstrates canine loyalty by testifying that a man like Faulkner never intended to do wrong, that Whitfield constantly taunted him about his business troubles, that he was driven to suicide. A note is given to the defense attorney asking that Andre not be put on the stand until the writer arrives at court, and Andre insists on taking the stand immediately.

There she describes her relationship with Faulkner, how he made love to her the first day she came to his Stockholm office looking for work, how she became his mistress, how he loved her until he died. She says he married Nancy Lee only because her father would not otherwise extend a $10 million loan, which he could not pay on time. He did promise to dismiss Karen, but all along he planned to return to her. When Whitfield reneged on the extension, she and Faulkner forged Whitfield's signature to $25 million worth of stock securities, but it was not enough. She is about to testify that Faulkner preferred death to poverty and that he committed suicide when "Guts" Regan enters the courtroom and blurts out that Faulkner is dead. This is apparently a surprise to Andre, who suddenly faints.

Act 3 begins with the conclusion of Andre's testimony. She now admits that she and Faulkner faked the suicide. Faulkner sent Whitfield's millions to South America, "Guts" found a corpse the same size as Faulkner, they brought it to the penthouse "drunk," and Faulkner changed clothes with it and left. Regan was to fly him to Buenes Aires, and Andre to meet him there. "Bjorn never thought of things as right or wrong," she says. "To him, it was only: you can or you can't. He always could." So could Andre, who threw a corpse over the balcony.

Regan picks up the story. He arrived at the airstrip to find the getaway plane gone. He did find a limousine hidden in the trees nearby. In the morning a man returned to it, disheveled, and gave him a check for $5,000 to keep quiet. Submitted as evidence, the check was dated January 17th and signed "John Graham Whitfield." Regan says he went looking for Faulkner in Argentina, returned to the states to look for the plane, and only yesterday found it in New Jersey. A charred skeleton in the burned shell, which he says was Faulkner, had been shot twice before the plane was torched. "Guts" admits to the prosecutor that he loves Karen Andre, that it was he who was kissing her at Faulkner's wedding, and that he would do anything, including lie or kill, to save her.

John Graham Whitfield testifies that Regan's story is a complete fabrication and explains that he hired Regan and paid him $5,000 to guard his daughter the day after Faulkner was killed. He knew nothing about the money sent to Argentina. Jungquist blurts out that he told Whitfield about the money, unaware that he was sentencing his patron to death; but the prosecution says that it is one man's word against another, and the defense rests.

The jury is taken away, where a simple majority is needed to convict or acquit. They may either decide that a jilted Karen Andre, in a fit of jealousy, forged a suicide note and pushed her lover (who was drunk or drugged) to his death. Not likely, given what the jury has seen and heard. Or they may decide that Faulkner and

Andre concocted an elaborate hoax, that a dead man's body was thrown from the balcony, that Faulkner is either still alive or dead at the hands of Whitfield or Regan. Rand thought it obvious that Andre was innocent—innocent of murder, certainly not of perjury. Yet her juries, perhaps enjoying punishing this bad girl, found Andre guilty forty percent of the time. Fortunately Rand provided two endings: if not guilty, Andre thanks the jury and is released without a word said about her perjury; if guilty, she announces there will be no appeal, that the verdict has saved her the effort to commit suicide. Nothing is said about arresting Whitfield or Regan, and no one suggests performing autopsies to discover just who is and who is not dead.

The real question for Rand was not who was dead and who was guilty but who in the cast had the superior "sense of life." When she published the script in 1968, she defined "sense of life" as a person's "emotional, subconsciously integrated appraisal of man's relationship to existence." Her play contrasted that of Bjorn Faulkner (and Karen Andre) with that of John Graham Whitfield (and Nancy Lee). The events and characters were not to be taken literally; they were intended merely to dramatize "certain fundamental psychological characteristics, deliberately isolated and emphasized in order to convey a single abstraction: the character's attitude toward life." The play, she said, should be considered "romantic symbolism."[7]

Bjorn Faulkner and Karen Andre represented passionate self-assertiveness, self-confidence, ambition, audacity, and independence from social norms. John Graham Whitfield and Nancy Lee represented conventionality, servility, envy, hatred, and lust for power over other people. Rand knew from the start that audiences would mistake her message, think the play a murder mystery, enjoy "the gimmick," and go home unenlightened; but she wrote it, offered it, and suffered embarrassment in order to build a foundation for a career that would attract an audience to understand.

She always felt she had to defend what people called the play's immorality. Bjorn Faulkner, she explained in the 1968 preface, is not an ideal man. She was not ready in 1933 to portray the ideal man. Howard Roark was five years away from birth. Bjorn Faulkner is already dead when the play begins and is seen only through the eyes of those who loved and hated him. This is Karen Andre's story, and it portrays "a woman's feeling for her ideal man." It is Karen Andre and not Bjorn Faulkner who is on trial; and we are told to

judge her only by the standards of loyalty. She cannot be immoral—
or guilty—even if the life she lives is immoral, even if she is guilty.
Because Faulkner was a man of supreme self-confidence, because he
won and held the love of a woman like Karen Andre, it is irrelevant
whether or not he is a crook.

Night of January 16th was a popular success and brought Rand
the fame she so desperately desired. Yet it does not bear close
scrutiny, and it does not really convey the "senses of life" Rand
thought it did. In the final analysis, despite its significance for her
career, it is held together by an enormously attractive woman and
a gimmick. It is great entertainment, but it is not philosophy. Rand
would gladly have sacrificed the first for the second, and in her later
fiction she would consciously do just that.

We the Living

While *Night of January 16th* entertained without indoctrinating,
We the Living indoctrinated without entertaining. Novels "with a
message," whatever the message, often fail to achieve the level of
great fiction. Rand believed that this novel was long rejected by
publishers and ill-treated by critics because it told the truth about
the Soviet system, when in fact it was rejected and criticized because
it was preachy. Those who bought and continue to buy it liked,
and still like, Rand's sermon.

We the Living was written between 1931 and 1933 and published
in 1936. Thus it is a contemporary of "Red Pawn" and *Night of
January 16th*. Its central figure, Kira (for Cyrus) Argounova, is a
woman, as are the central figures Joan in "Red Pawn" and Karen
Andre in *Night of January 16th*. But in this novel Rand at last
attempts to create a male hero, not one seen through a woman's
eyes, not one already dead, and not one but two. Leo Kovalensky
and Andrei Tagonov are not yet Howard Roark and John Galt, but
they are vital first steps in that direction. It may come as a shock
to those who think of Rand as an anticommunist to learn that the
most admirable men in "Red Pawn" and *We the Living* are both
communists.

In her preface to the 1958 edition, Rand wrote that *We the Living*
is "as near an autobiography as I will ever write."[8] Not literally,
she hastened to add, but intellectually. Kira is a student of engineering while Rand studied history; Kira wants to build, Rand

wanted to write; and Kira dies trying to escape Russia, while Rand
escaped and lived a full life. But Rand, like Kira, knew from
childhood that she hated the communist system, from the moment
it told her that man exists for the state. And so to a large extent,
though we can never know how faithfully she portrayed her university friends and experiences, this story is Rand's pilgrimage.

It will be the last time she sets a story in Russia, unless we
surmise that Russia is the backdrop for the nebulous and futuristic
Anthem. The "great" novels, *The Fountainhead* and *Atlas Shrugged*,
are both set in America. *We the Living* is the only one of her novels
with an atmosphere akin to that of Boris Pasternak's *Doctor Zhivago*.
Yet Rand always said that this is not really a story about Russia or
even about the Soviet system as such. To her it was a story about
man against the state, its theme universal, its philosophy timeless.
To her it happened in any state at any time where and when men
and women are enslaved and made to serve the common good.

The 1958 paperback edition, which most people read today,
contains revisions. Rand explained that she changed certain language
to make it sound more American, less stilted, easier for the casual
reader to follow. Her English, she admitted, was in 1933 still a
bit uncertain. Yet as she reread it twenty-five years later she found
her original philosophy of life unchanged, and she was pleased at
how well she had been able to express it. While she improved her
English, she was unable to improve her philosophy. It was essentially
unchanged through the course of her adult life.

The story of *We the Living* begins in 1922 as the Argounova
family—Kira, her parents, her older sister—return to Petrograd
from four years in the Crimea. Her father, once a textile manufac-
turer, has lost his business during the revolution and is a broken
man. The escape to the south has proven futile. Kira, who has never
had a boyfriend but who dreams of a Viking she once read about
in a novel, wants to be an architect. Above her bed, like an icon,
hangs a picture of a New York skyscraper. She does not believe in
God, but she believes in man.

As soon as she enters the Technological Institute she meets a
young communist leader named Andrei Taganov and spends her
spare daylight hours with him, while she spends nights with a
mysterious young resister named Leo Kovalensky. Andrei cautions
her to keep quiet about her opposition to the Party. He sees in
communism hope for the downtrodden, for people like his father

who died in a czarist camp in Siberia. Kira argues with him that the state should exist for the people, not the people for the state, and that she will never be reconciled to the idea of sacrificing the individual for "the common good." The other man, Leo, tells her not to hope for things to get better. His father was a great captain in the czar's fleet who was blinded during the war and then executed by the communists as a subversive. When she tells him her dream of building skyscrapers, he asks her why she bothers. When she replies that she wants to be admired, he warns her that it is a curse "to be able to look higher than you're allowed to reach" (W, 74).

Thus in the opening chapters Kira becomes involved with two men, one intellectually, the other both intellectually and physically, whose backgrounds and philosophies differ not only from each other but also from her own. She has a stronger commitment than Leo, though it is to a different faith, and a stronger resolve than Andrei, though it is to a different cause. As in earlier works, Rand's woman, though she pretends to worship maleness, is superior to Rand's men. One wonders what inner conflict she was trying to resolve as she created women superior to men, while forcing them to bow to male dominance.

While Kira keeps her relationships with Andrei platonic, she makes an ill-fated attempted to flee Russia with Leo and gives up her virginity to him in midflight. After they are caught and then released because an official fondly remembers Leo's father, Kira goes to live with him in his father's old apartment. Leo has the body of a Greek god and the soul of a Greek hero. Although he hates the Soviet regime, he works for the government, translating foreign novels that demonstrate the evils of capitalism. When this work is done, he is forced to do manual labor and becomes ill. Kira is expelled from the Technological Institute for bourgeois attitudes. Leo must go away, to the Crimea, if he is to live; and to save him Kira pretends to love Andrei to secure money from him to send Leo to a sanatorium in Yalta.

Once again, as in "Red Pawn," Rand makes a woman give herself to one man in order to save another, again to a communist to save a lover. This seems to be the only type of self-sacrifice she ever approved. Perhaps to a greater degree than in "Red Pawn," this communist turns out to be a more admirable person than the man the woman saved. The entire second half of We the Living, in fact, deals with the corruption of Leo and the heroism of Andrei. Despite

her desire to condemn the system that Leo despises and for which
Andrei works so faithfully, despite pages and pages of commentary
and dialogue aimed at making her anti-Soviet point, she permits
Andrei's dedication to the revolution to ennoble him, while she
permits Leo's efforts to make money by subverting the system to
pull him ever deeper into disrepute. One has to wonder if Ayn
Rand, the self-described "radical for capitalism," was fully aware
of what this novel and "Red Pawn" were saying. In her own defense
she would probably have pointed out how depraved she made all
the other communists in the story. She might particularly have
singled out the case of Kira's cousin Victor, a man totally without
scruples who sees in the Party a path to power over other men and
its subsequent comforts.

Leo returns from the Crimea physically well but still spiritually
tortured. Although Kira has been sleeping with Andrei and working
as a guide in the Museum of the Revolution by his grace, she moves
back in with Leo. Before long Leo is prospering in a job of his own,
working a store stocked by a smuggler who happens to be the lover
of a woman he met in the south. The communist system is being
reborn in rewards given to good party members, certain chosen
professions valuable to the party are being given priorities, and
young people are denouncing relatives, not for corruption but for
deviation from party dogma. Rand paints a touching picture—
possibly autobiographical—of a pair of young lovers separated forever when the boy is sent to Siberia for dissident behavior. In this
atmosphere Leo's cynical exploitations are rewarded, while Andrei's
faith in the new regime is shaken. Oddly enough, Kira is more
attracted to Leo in his "fallen" state than she was earlier and even
proposes marriage to him while refusing to escape the country with
the more admirable and honest Andrei.

Throughout this ordeal Leo and Andrei do not know that they
share Kira's affection. Andrei sets out to expose corruption without
knowing he is closing in on Leo. He is warned by Party members
that to continue his crusade will injure the cause; but he is too
honest to sweep matters under the rug. In his investigations he
discovers that Kira is living with Leo and that she only pretended
to love him (Andrei), used him, to help another man. Kira shows
no remorse for what she has done, and Andrei does not condemn
her. Instead, nobler still, he promises to save Leo from the net he
has cast.

At a Party gathering Andrei delivers a speech that will end his career. "Every man worth calling a man lives for himself," he says. "The one who doesn't—doesn't live at all. You cannot change it. You cannot change it because that's the way man is born, alone, complete, an end in himself. No laws, no party, no G.P.U. will ever kill that thing in man which knows how to say 'I' " (W, 392). This of course sounds more like Howard Roark than the Andrei earlier in the novel; but it is supposed to show the change that Kira and his recent experience have had on him.

He blackmails a Party official to secure Leo's release, assures Leo that he and Kira are only friends, and takes his own life. While misguided before he met Kira, Andrei was all his life a noble person, dedicated to noble causes, far superior to men who sought power or creature comforts. His spirit emerges victorious, even in death. In later novels he is represented by Howard Roark and John Galt.

Again the heroine Kira is boldly honest. She admits to Leo that she has been Andrei's mistress, whereupon he announces that he has decided to go away with another woman. Kira moves back to her parents' house, applies for a passport to leave Russia, and is turned down. It then becomes a matter of living her life out under a system she despises or risking it once more in an attempt to escape. While trying to cross the far northern frontier wearing white clothing in the snow, she is shot by a border guard who takes her for a rabbit. She dies thinking of the things that might have but will not be.

Ideal

We the Living is pessimistic. Those with integrity die, while those without it live to inherit the earth. *Night of January 16th*, admittedly lighter entertainment than *We the Living*, at least leaves its vibrant heroine alive at play's end. In both stories, however, hero and heroine are victims of collectivist society, one hypocritical America and the other socialist Russia. It is obvious that in 1934, before he play's success on Broadway and before her novel had found a publisher, Rand was in an emotional trough. That year she wrote another play, never produced, called *Ideal*; other than its slightly hopeful ending it is an exercise in pessimism.

Rand considered herself an idealist, and by 1934 she had come to the conclusion that her adopted country was in its own way as unsympathetic to idealism as the country she had abandoned. Both the hero and the heroine of the new play are idealists, and they are both made aliens by American pragmatism. Despite its contrived "happy" ending, it clearly demonstrates that things never turn out well for idealists. In his 1984 introduction to the play Leonard Peikoff wrote that this "bad mood" and pessimism were "untypical" of Rand, that it was only a temporary aberration (*E,* 184). A close look at her career, however, would seem to show that from 1929 on her fiction remained essentially scornful, even when she tried to be constructive, and that while she was later able to provide more positive resolutions than this play's death of an innocent, she remained for the rest of her life a pessimist, and as such an avenger.

The story of *Ideal* was suggested to Rand by a friend who desperately wanted to meet a certain famous movie star. The remark led Rand to ask herself what would happen if such a star, so admired by so many people, were to come to her fans one by one and ask their help in time of need. Would they respond? Would they even recognize her? Rand found little in her own recent experience to indicate that people would help. Later she claimed that she had received no help at all as she learned American ways—while conveniently forgetting certain important exceptions. Later still she argued that she had not expected any help, that a person should neither ask nor give help—unless to do so would be beneficial to the one giving it. But at this time she could still be outraged that Kay Gonda, accused of murder, would appeal to devoted fans and be denied and betrayed.

The fans whose devotion Kay tests are an intriguing array of characters, and for their sakes alone it is a pity the play was never produced. There is Dwight Langley, an artist, a Platonist who is convinced that beauty is an ideal no human artist can reach. His emphasis in on characteristics, not character, and while he knows every detail of Kay's face, he fails to recognize the woman herself. Had he been an Aristotelian, had he believed that ideas can be known by human reason, he would have recognized, come to the rescue, and claimed the love of the woman he so much admired.

There is also Claude Ignatius Hix, a fundamentalist preacher. His fails to be a Good Samaritan because his religion tells him that earthly suffering is good, since it leads to heavenly rewards. Well fed and without apparent discomfort himself, he sits back and mouths pious platitudes. Had he been a Randian atheist, he would have known that human suffering is without meaning, and he would have come to Kay's relief. He would have had his reward here and now, the only place possible really, and helping another person would have been a means of self-fulfillment.

The only bright spot in this list of fair-weather fans is young Johnnie Dawes. His idealism, as strong as Kay's, has made him a misfit in modern society. He alone recognizes, understands, and appreciates Kay; and he alone realizes that it is in his own self-interest to help her. He confesses to the crime she is accused of committing and takes his own life, one of several Rand characters who sacrifice themselves for others. It is difficult to reconcile these characters with Rand's denunciations of self-sacrifice, except perhaps to note that the sacrifices are for selfish reasons, to fulfill ideals without which life would not have been worth living anyway.

At any rate, in Johnnie's act Kay is both saved and given a ray of hope. It may be that in 1934 Rand was herself looking for a man like Johnnie. She may have thought she found him in A. H. Woods, the man who bought *Penthouse Legend* and took it to Broadway. Sadly, however, her "Johnnie" turned out to be a crook, and she was so embittered by the experience that it would be a long time before she or one of her female characters was in a good mood.

Anthem

Rand's drive was born of anger; but anger cannot provide a person with a message. The germ of what would be her message can be seen in the passionate human struggles of her early stories, in the bold assertions of *Night of January 16th,* and in the denunciations of collective morality and herd mentality of *We the Living;* but it is only in *Anthem,* her brief second novel, that her message takes on its clear and distinctive form. While the players for her two great later novels are still embryos in this dystopia, *Anthem* is the overture for the Rand symphony composed of *The Fountainhead* and *Atlas Shrugged.*

Anthem was born an outline for a play, jotted down in spare moments while Rand was at university in Petrograd, and it would always retain a theatrical quality. It became a novel in narrative form thirteen years later, in Connecticut during the summer of 1937. It was published in 1938, not in the United States, where it found no publisher, but in England. Only in 1946 did it appear under an American imprint, and when it did Rand wrote, "I have lifted its face," meaning she had made changes of language, "but not its spine or spirit."[9] The latter were from the start as she wanted them.

The story is written in the form of a journal kept by a man of the future living in a totalitarian state, a man whose name is Equality 7–2521. He admits that it is dangerous to keep such a record because "there is no transgression blacker than to do or think alone" (*A*, 11). So says the Council of Vocations, which determines each man's work, in a state where a man must say "we" instead of "I" when referring to himself. Over the portal of the Palace of the World Council are the words:

> We are one in all and all in one.
> There are no men but only the Great We,
> One, indivisible and forever.

The Great Truth taught to all is "that all men are one and that there is no will save the will of all men together" (*A*, 14–15).

Equality 7–2521 lived to the age of five in the Home of the Infants and from five to fifteen in the Home of the Students, where he was taught the rules of collectivist society. Now that he is grown, and both taller and smarter than other men, he is a Streetsweeper. It is a job that for years he considered proper because he dared question the Council of Vocations. He had selfishly wanted to be a Scholar. At forty he will retire to the Home of the Useless, where he will be one of the Ancient Ones.

In recent days he has kept this journal to try to make sense of what is happening to him. He has made friends with another man, International 4–8818; and they have discovered a tunnel, a remnant of structures from Unmentionable Times, before the Great Rebirth when all dangerous books were burned. He has gone there to study manuscripts which he steals from the Clerks, to tinker with chemicals, and to dissect animals. All alone among men he is doing work that has no purpose except his own pleasure. He knows peace.

He has known women only during the Time of Mating; but through the daring of his newfound freedom he meets Liberty 5–3000, a laborer in the fields, and renames her Golden One. She is seventeen and has never been to the Palace of Mating. She renames him the Unconquered, the name Rand would later give to the play she adapted from *We the Living.* Out of his love for her comes a desire to discover and say the Unspeakable Word, a word the Transgressor was burned at the stake for daring to say.

In the tunnel he mixes zinc and copper in a jar of brine and makes a powder that can turn the needle of a compass. He makes a light box in which a wire can be made to glow. He dares show his inventions to the World Council of Scholars, calling them "the key to the earth" and "the power of the sky," and the Scholars accuse him of trying to disturb the economic order. "What is not done collectively," they tell him, "cannot be good." They are afraid he might bankrupt the candle industry with his electricity (A, 81).

He is chased from the city and hides in the Uncharted Forest. Golden One follows and finds him; and together they wander until they find a house built by people in Unmentionable Times. He learns to hunt like a man, while she learns the pleasures of looking into a mirror, presumably like a woman. When he tells her that this is their place and that they will never share it with anyone, she says to her lord and master, "Your will be done" (A, 105).

He vows never again to say "we" because this word is "lime poured over men, which sets and hardens to stone." He says that from now forward his credo will be: "I am a man. This miracle of me is mine to own and keep, and mine to guard, and mine to use, and mine to kneel before" (A, 110). From a manuscript he has found in the house he takes the name Prometheus and gives to Golden One the name Gaea; for he is to be the source of light, while she is to be Mother Earth. He knows that the Transgressor has chosen him to be his intellectual heir. He will erect an electric barrier around his home and raise his son as a free man. He promises one day to go back to the city and bring like-minded man, fellow builders, to live with him in freedom behind his walls.

He concludes that men were first enslaved by gods and broke their chains, then by kings and broke them, then by a class structure and broke them to stand now on the threshold of freedom before being suddenly enslaved by the worship of "We." He ends his story by uttering the word that mean freedom, the word spoken by the Transgressor, the forbidden, sacred word: *Ego.* He is a man.

Anthem is a dystopia (a fantasy about the opposite of a perfect society)—written eleven years before George Orwell's *1984*—which contains the germ of a utopia, the one Prometheus promises to carve out of the Uncharted Forest. Rand's dystopia, a collectivist state, is a place of conformity and drudgery, without love, progress, or electricity. Her utopia will be a place where men hunt and women admire them, where "like-minded" men can relearn the glory of self-respect and self-assertion. A reader who is unwilling to suspend disbelief on a grand scale will find *Anthem* ridiculous. Rand fans have apparently been able to do so because for them this brief story is an icon. Prometheus prefigures Howard Roark and John Galt. The Uncharted Forest is Galt's Gulch. *Anthem* is an overture for the opera to come.

Think Twice

Rand wrote two more plays while she took notes and drew scenarios for *The Fountainhead,* the book that would someday bring her the fame and fortune she had sought. One play was an adaptation of her novel *We the Living,* the other a murder mystery called *Think Twice.* The adaptation, entitled *The Unconquered,* found a producer, despite a story line that publishers had found unappealing, due to the recent success of *Night of January 16th,* and opened on Broadway in February 1940. Rosamond Gilder wrote in *Theatre Arts* that *The Unconquered* smacked of nineteenth-century melodrama and seemed to depict more the French than the Russian Revolution.[10] Philip Hartung in *Commonweal* called it "a confused muddle in ten scenes trying to say that the human spirit cannot survive under collectivism." He labeled Rand's characters cardboard figures and suggested that for anti-Soviet sniping it would be better to see the Greta Garbo film *Ninotchka.*[11] *The Unconquered* quickly closed and never reopened.

Think Twice, also written in 1939, was never produced, perhaps because *The Unconquered* ended Rand's theatrical career forever, perhaps because it failed, despite its Nazi villain, to conform to the American zeitgeist of 1939. Rand's oversimplifications, charming in *Night of January 16th,* dramatic in later novels, seem silly in *Think Twice.* Here again, as in *Anthem,* she equates egoism with heroism and argues that altruism is the root of all evil. But here her characters are too weak to bear her message.

The altruist, Walter Breckenridge, gives things away—personal things, professional things—in order to gain power over the people who accept his gifts. He is, as the play begins, preparing to "give" the world, including America's enemies, his formula for capturing the energy of cosmic rays. The egoist, Steve Ingalls, Breckenridge's partner, is given to lines like "I like to make money. I think money is a wonderful thing. I don't see what's wrong with making a fortune—if you deserve it and people are willing to pay for what you offer them" (*E,* 275). To prevent Breckenridge from giving away the formula, he murders him. Adrienne Knowland, the female lead, has loved Ingalls for a long time but seems to desire him all the more when she learns of the murder. There is a happy ending. The murder is blamed on the Nazi, who in later revisions becomes a communist.

All in all this play is best forgotten. Even Rand did not mourn it. Much later she would admit that she could never have written mysteries because in them the egoist would inevitably have killed the altruist and gone free. She recognized how simplistic her philosophy was and the limitations it placed on her work. Yet she kept *Think Twice* close to her, revising it, sharing it with disciples, enjoying their vain attempts to solve the mystery before the final scene, perhaps hoping that it would someday be produced. It never was.

The Fountainhead

In 1937, as she worked in a New York architectural firm, Rand began formulating a story about a young builder. The novel required six years to complete—though most of it was written in 1942—and became her first best-seller. The builder was Howard Roark, the novel *The Fountainhead.*

Late in 1941, with the aid of Archibald Ogden, Rand signed a contract with Bobbs-Merrill to complete a manuscript that was then only one-fourth done. She worked throughout the next year, and met her deadline, finishing the manuscript by the beginning of 1943. It was reviewed sparingly and gingerly. Lorine Pruette in the *New York Times Book Review* complimented Rand for writing a novel of ideas, something different for a woman. Although she was disturbed by Rand's false dichotomy between selfishness and altruism, she admired this hymn to individualism and praised Rand for writing so "brilliantly, beautifully, bitterly."[12] N. L. Rothman in the *Saturday Review* found the coupling of collectivism and dictatorship too pat, but he admired the character Howard Roark and decided that Rand's "satire" on American life, all 754 pages, was not a page too long.[13]

Readers apparently agreed. Sales grew steadily, despite weak reviews and little publicity, as months passed. The book sold more copies in 1944 than in 1943 and yet more in 1945, when it spent twenty-six weeks on the best-seller list. It returned to the best-seller list in 1949, when the film version of the story was released and Bobbs-Merrill reissued it at the original hardback price of three dollars. To date its sales, including paperback editions, are nearing the three million mark.

The Fountainhead hardly mentions politics or economics, despite the fact that it was born in the 1930s. Nor does it deal with world affairs, although it was written during World War II. It is about one man against the system, and it does not permit other matters to intrude. It is set in America between the wars; but Howard Roark knows only architecture, and this is his story. Although Rand dedicated the novel to Frank O'Connor, she wrote in a preface that reads like a dedication: "I offer my profound gratitude to the great profession of architecture and its heroes who have given us some of the highest expressions of man's genius, yet have remained unknown, undiscovered by the majority of men."[14] This feast is not for politicians and economists, only for builders.

It is graduation day in 1922 at the Stanton Institute of Technology. Peter Keating (which rhymes with *cheating, bleating*) has just delivered his valedictory, while junior Howard Roark (hard rock that he is) has just been expelled. Yet Keating is confused, while Roark is cheerfully sure of himself. Roark tells the dean who has expelled him that he should have left the place years before, that he cares not at all what other men think of him or his work, that he does not care whether they think of him at all. Later that day Keating comes to him, afraid to make his own decision, asking Roark whether he should accept a position with the Francon Architectural Firm in New York City or go for further study in Europe. In these first pages we see the individualist and the second-hander, the man who thinks for himself and the man who does not, and Rand will play them off against each other for another 700 pages.

Roark and Keating go to the city, which is about as much like New York as is Superman's Metropolis. Keating plays up to Francon and quickly climbs over his follow workers to the top of the corporate ladder. Roark takes a job as assistant to Henry Cameron, the first man to build a skyscraper, who in the "neo-classical revival" is now destitute. When Cameron asks Roark why he decided to be an

architect, Roark explains that it is because he does not believe in
God: "Because I love this earth. That's all I love. I don't like the
shape of things on this earth. I want to change them" (*F*, 45).

Keating outmaneuvers other architects to become Francon's chief
designer; but when he needs a design for an important competition
he goes to Roark, persuades him to do the work, and passes Roark's
design off as his own. Meantime Roark and Cameron sink lower in
sales, fall further behind, and Cameron advises his young assistant
to sell out, to give the public what it wants, the way that Gail
Wynand, owner of the *Banner* newspaper, does. He is actually test-
ing Roark's resolve; and he is pleased when Roark vows that he
would rather starve. He recognizes in this young rebel a man of
great spirit. He knows that eventually he will be a winner.

Gail Wynand's *Banner* features a column on architecture called
"One Small Voice" by the famous "altruist" Ellsworth Toohey (which
of course rhymes with either *hoohey* or *foohey*), author of the best-
selling book *Sermons in Stone.* Ellsworth Toohey, like Walter Breckenridge in *Think Twice,* claims to be a humanitarian, but in reality
he covets power over the humanity he claims to serve. Toohey argues
that architecture, the queen of the arts, should reflect the will of
the people. Another *Banner* column, on interior decorating called
"Your House," is written by Guy Francon's daughter Dominique
(dominant), a rich lady in a perpetual snit against the pedestrian
tastes of her society, an idealist alienated by the shallow conventions
of her day. Peter Keating's designs receive praise from Toohey and
scorn from Dominique, while Howard Roark neither knows nor is
known by either one.

Cameron collapses and is forced to retire, and Roark finds himself
out in the cold. Keating, seeing in Roark his Sidney Carton, has
him hired at the Francon firm; but when Roark predictably refuses
his first assignment, to work on a joint project, he is predictably
fired. For months he is without work until hired as the resident
"modernist" stylist by a firm desiring versatility, only to go over
his boss's head to sell an idea to a client and be fired once again.
But the client, Austen Heller, is so impressed that he hires Roark
as an independent agent and gives him full rein to build his home
as he pleases. The establishment officially ignores the resultant work
of genius but in private derides it as "the booby hatch." Howard
Roark is not of this world.

Keating meets and falls in love with Dominique, despite the fact that he has promised to marry Toohey's niece, but Dominique treats him like the secondhander he is. Soon she is involved in a dispute between her boss, Gail Wynand, whom she has never met, and a group of landowners over a move to raze a slum. Wynand wants the land, in the neighborhood where he grew up, to build a new *Banner* building. Dominique writes a series of articles on living conditions there, offending slumlords, social workers, and her boss. She is not worried. "It would be terrible to have a job I enjoyed and did not want to lose," she says. To her freedom is: "To ask nothing, to expect nothing. To depend on nothing" (*F,* 148). She begins dating Keating simply because she despises him so. Dominique is unique.

Meanwhile Roark loses assignments he might have received by his refusal to compromise his standards. Even his benefactor Austen Heller calls him a self-centered monster, all the more monstrous because he does not know he is one. Keating again comes to him for help in designing a movie company building. It wins the $10 million competition, and Keating returns to pay Roark for keeping quiet about the deal; but instead Roark offers to pay Keating for remaining silent.

Keating asks Dominique to marry him, but she refuses and goes away to her father's Connecticut farm to reasses her life. At the same time Roark is so desperate for work that he takes a job in a quarry on the same estate. Roark and Dominique have never met, but fate is about to arrange it. Even as he heads for his Connecticut exile, it is evident that Roark will return, that he will be victorious, and that justice will be done.

One day Dominique rides down from her father's mansion to the quarry and sees a man with orange hair drilling granite. In his face she sees "the abstraction of strength made visible." She is unable to forget this man with the large, irresistible drill, and she purposely breaks the slab of marble before her fireplace so that she can have him come to repair it. After only a few minutes together they recognize their mutual love-contempt, and Roark rapes her. It is an act of scorn, performed by a male who has heretofore seemed sexless, against a woman who has found sex tasteless. It is just what has been missing from Dominique's life. "One gesture of tenderness from him," Rand says, "and she would have remained cold, untouched by the thing done to her body. But the act of a master taking shameful, contemptuous possession of her was the kind of

rapture she had wanted" (F, 231). The next time she calls for him
he has gone, and she is even more fascinated when no one can tell
her his name.

He has returned to the city, to build a home for Roger Enright.
Dominique admires this house, and at a reception for its designer
she learns that he is the man who had raped her. She writes an
article ridiculing the house, but admits to herself that it is too good
for this world, that she is merely assisting public opinion to bring
it down. The storm her article stirs costs Roark an assured second
commission, and Dominique goes to his apartment to gloat, only
to be wonderfully raped a second time.

Meanwhile Ellsworth Toohey gains power in the world of architecture by organizing the Council of American Builders, with Keating as chairman, to encourage the kind of humanistic architecture
that creates brotherhood among men. "Only when you can feel
contempt for your own priceless little ego," he tells his eager followers, "only then can you achieve the true, broad peace of selflessness, the merging of your spirit with the vast collective spirit
of mankind" (F, 320). He dreams of controlling that collective
spirit.

Out of jealously for Roark's individualistic spirit, Toohey rec-
ommends him to build a "Temple to the Human Spirit" for a man
he knows will hate Roark's work. Roark surprisingly accepts the
odd commission and builds the temple while his patron is out of
the country. He hires a young sculptor to do a nude figure of
Dominique as a centerpiece for the building. Toohey cleverly turns
the patron against the building, convincing him that it is an offense
to decency, and persuades him to sue Roark. Thus begins another
Rand trial. Roark offers no defense and loses. At Toohey's suggestion
the patron turns the building into a home for subnormal children.

Out of pure disgust with herself and the world in general, Dominique decides to marry Peter Keating. On her wedding night she
passively submits to his passion and then goes off to sleep with
Roark. She tells Roark that his buildings are mountains that threaten
moles, that the world must destroy him to keep from feeling inferior,
and that she has decided to destroy herself first. Roark replies that
the world will not destroy him or her and that one day she will be
his forever.

Next we meet Gail Wynand, a man with qualities like Roark
mixed with those of Keating. Wynand has risen to the top, but he

will be reduced to oblivion. He is perhaps Rand's only truly classical tragic figure. A self-made man, the son of a longshoreman but with a hint of aristocratic blood, he has built a financial empire from nothing. Without schooling he worked his way up in the newspaper business; and with the help of thugs he gained control of the *Banner*. Along the way he learned that the way to succeed is to "give people what they want," and in William Randolph Hearst fashion he creates sensational stories for public consumption. He feels no need for integrity until he meets Howard Roark.

Wynand dreams of building a community on Long Island; and Ellsworth Toohey, playing with fire, sends him the statue of Dominique Francon. Although she has worked for him, Dominique and Wynand have never met, and Toohey introduces them. When she shows him neither respect nor affection, Wynand wants her for his own. Toohey gladly works out an arrangement in which Wynand takes Dominique on a two-month cruise in exchange for giving the Long Island commission to husband Peter Keating. Peter and Dominique agree to this unsavory scheme, Peter out of greed, Dominique because she does not care where she is. On the cruise they do not make love because they want to do what is not expected of them: abnormal behavior is to wait until after marriage to have sexual relations.

Peter Keating agrees to a divorce. On her way to Nevada Dominique stops in the Ohio town where Roark is working. All that excites her sexually now is his contempt and watching skyscrapers being erected. He sends her on her way. She marries Wynand and moves into his glass-walled penthouse, where the two of them share a mutually passionate contempt.

There is a strange nonphysical homoerotic relationship between Roark and Wynand, a love affair that dwarfs any heterosexual affairs in Rand's fiction. Wynand asks Roark to build a home for Dominique, a fortress and a temple, to protect and enshrine her. During planning sessions they come to feel strong mutual attraction. Wynand admires Roark's honesty, independence, integrity; while Roark finds in Wynand a native artistic sensitivity he has never known in a man of power. As they view the emerging erection from a distance, Rand interprets their vision: "The stems were dry and naked, but there was a quality of spring in the cheerful insolence of their upward thrust, the stirring of a self-assertive purpose" (*F*, 595).

Wynand takes Roark on a five-month cruise, leaving Dominique behind, and one day tells him that the statue to the human spirit should have been of Roark, not Dominique. Roark wins Wynand's heart as well as his respect when he declares that he does not want to be a symbol for anything. Dominique seems happy to have the two men in her life spend so much time together and even says that making love to Wynand is much better now that he spends his days talking with Roark. When she suggests that Wynand worships Roark, Wynand describes Roark as his hair shirt. At last he takes Roark to Hell's Kitchen, his old neighborhood, and shows him the block where he wants Roark one day to build the Wynand Building. This is the highest favor he can bestow.

All this time Peter Keating is obsessed with making a return to the public favor he lost with his divorce and decides to submit a bid to build a low-cost housing project called Cortlandt. He begs Roark for a design, and Roark agrees to do it if Keating swears not to alter his plan. When Keating proves too weak to keep his promise and stop the changes from being made, Roark plots with Dominique to take vengeance. She distracts the guard while he sets explosives and with one bang destroys his own building.

Roark is arrested and refuses to offer excuses. Wynand throws the *Banner* behind his cause, the public turns against Wynand, and Toohey decides it is time to lead a coup. He attacks Roark, Wynand fires him, and he leads a workers' strike against the paper. Faced with financial ruin, Wynand gives in and permits an editorial to be written under his name condemning Roark for what he did. Dominique conspires to let the press know that she is now sleeping with Roark, out on bail raised by Wynand, and when Wynand sues for divorce he is treated like a martyr. Once again he is rich and powerful, but he has bought these things at the cost of his integrity, and he is a broken man.

At his trial Howard Roark serves as his own defense attorney. He calls no witnesses. He admits freely that he blew up the Cortlandt, which he also admits he designed. "I gave it to you," he says simply. "I destroyed it" (*F,* 742). He defends only one thing, his own ego. The egoist does not live for others, he says, nor does he live off them. He asks no one to live for or off him. This is the only true basis for a brotherhood of man. The jury finds him not guilty.

The rest is history—and happy history at that. Roark gets to rebuild Cortlandt in his own image. He marries Dominique—his first marriage, her third. Wynand sells the *Banner,* and Toohey begins plotting how to control his new boss. Wynand now gives the commission to build the Wynand Building to Roark with only one directive: "Build it as a monument to that spirit which is yours . . . and could have been mine" (*F,* 751). In the final scene "Mrs. Roark" comes to the building site and rides the elevator up the erection Roark is making for Wynand, up past the pinnacles of banks, the crowns of courthouses, the spires of churches, to the waiting figure of Howard Roark, the hard rock of egoism. Economic, political, and religious institutions are all insignificant when compared to the heroic man dedicated to magnificent erections.

The Fountainhead is quite a novel, perhaps the best Ayn Rand wrote. It is not as simple as it first appears, and it is more important than its detractors think, although not as important as Rand fans imagine. Nora Ephron, who wrote a retrospective on it in 1968, on the twenty-fifth anniversary of its publication, felt that she had completely missed its point when she read it in college. After re-reading it she concluded that "it is better read when one is young enough to miss the point."[15] *The Fountainhead* advocates chaos by romancing anarchy, sadomasochism, and infidelity. It appeals to bored, frustrated, angry young people, particularly those with un-earned money and unrealized talent. Whatever its merits or de-merits, it will continue to sell—and to form and confirm the prejudices of young Americans—into the foreseeable future.

Rand finished the screenplay for *The Fountainhead* a year after the book was published; but the war delayed movie production and release until 1949. It was not a success. Critics found it ridiculously preachy and predictable. Gary Cooper was too old and typecast to play Howard Roark. Raymond Massey as Gail Wynand proved ineffective in his part. Patricia Neal as Dominique, chosen at the last minute to replace Barbara Stanwyck, was effective but could not alone save one of King Vidor's few failures. Neal remembered thirty-five years later how her fellow actors avoided her after the premiere. She now says with faint praise that it perhaps plays better today than it did in 1949, perhaps because it is old enough to be recognized as the oddity it was even then.[16]

Rand's script captured the essence of the novel too well. Her message, when force-fed in a two-hour film, is revolting. Gary Cooper as Howard Roark made her point forcefully, eloquently, and ad nauseam. In several soliloquies he drove home her thesis that only by living for himself can a man achieve anything for mankind, that self-sacrifice breaks a man's spirit, and that "the man who works for others for nothing is a slave." Although Cooper behind a drafting board seemed about as convincing as Frank Lloyd Wright on a horse, he was true to the letter and spirit of Ayn Rand.

Atlas Shrugged

Rand was undisturbed by the way lesser mortals criticized the film. She was already at work on what she would later consider her true masterpiece, the largest and last of her novels, *Atlas Shrugged*. It took nine years to complete, ran to 1,168 pages, and ended her career in fiction. She called it her finest work, relegating *The Fountainhead* to the role of preview to the main feature, quoting it as if it were scripture.

Publisher Bennett Cerf warned the public that *Atlas Shrugged* would "hit with the force of a sledge-hammer," and reviewers agreed, praising it for its power, condemning it for its blunt ferocity. Patricia Donegan in *Commonweal* found it a "cumbersome, lumbering vehicle in which characterization, plot and reality are subordinated to the author's expression of a personal philosophy."[17] She was disgusted by Rand's "talent" for portraying her good guys as "beautiful, clear-eyed and intelligent" while giving all her bad guys "flabby jowls" and "bloodshot eyes."

Richard McLaughlin in *American Mercury* praised her for providing a much needed polemic against the loss of personal liberty, the increase in bureaucratic mumbo-jumbo, and the sociopolitical collectivist consensus of the day; but he called this "leviathan" of a novel a staggering answer to conservative prayers. Where it should have argued with reason it shouted wildly. Its characters were Byzantine mosaics of allegorical figures. He sniped that since Rand was "first and foremost a skillful polemicist, it may be asking too much to expect Miss Rand to have a literary style." Yet he compared her to Harriet Beecher Stowe and her book to *Uncle Tom's Cabin*. Both women and both books had messages worth hearing.[18]

Granville Hicks in the *New York Times Book Review* found both style and content offensive. Rand howled in the ear, banged on the head, and delivered interminable harangues of hate.[19] A reviewer for *Time* credited her with a good imagination but found it unfortunately tied to a ludicrous naïveté that would make intelligent readers laugh. *Atlas Shrugged* had "the blue-tinted fluorescent light of literary unreality; the dogged logic with which the illogical is propped up; the melodramatic simplicity that requires no scorecard to tell heroes from villains."[20] But the harshest criticism came from Whittaker Chambers. "Randian Man, like Marxian Man," he wrote in *National Review,* "is made the center of a godless world." From every page of her novel "a voice can be heard, from painful necessity, commanding: 'To a gas chamber—go!' "[21] Rand would never again have a good word for William F. Buckley or his magazine.

Much of the criticism, however, was gentle. Donald Malcolm wrote in the *New Yorker* that Rand's warning to Americans not to abandon factories, technology, and the profit motive was like admonishing water not to run uphill.[22] Helen Beal Woodward, writing for *Saturday Review,* called her good guys "mannequins" and her bad guys the finest assortment of straw men ever demolished in print. *Atlas Shrugged* was the daydream of a girl who enters a man's world with one hand running a railroad and the other reducing strong men to canine adoration.[23] A *Newsweek* reviewer allowed that the clarion call to abandon the Christian faith, return to raw capitalism, and forsake majority rule, despite the bombast, would crumble no walls.[24]

Despite the negative conclusions of the reviews, the book was being reviewed. It was also selling faster than Rand's earlier books. It is to date, despite its size, price, and verbiage, her best-selling work. *The Fountainhead* had avoided politics and economics, but *Atlas Shrugged* made them central. What Rand had to say seems to have been immensely appealing and explains why the book is still selling today.

Atlas Shrugged is the story of four heroes and one heroine. The men are three former college classmates, the Argentine Francisco d'Anconia, the Scandinavian Ragnar Danneskjöld, and the American John Galt, plus the American steel king Henry Rearden, who is in many ways like Howard Roark. The woman, who is at last Ayn Rand in a good mood, is the irrepressible and unforgettable Dagny Taggart. Played off against these four brave, honest, and heroic men and one intelligent, single-minded woman is an array of villains, enemies of individualism and free enterprise, personified by the big-hearted, small-brained altruist and collectivist Wesley Mouch.

The action takes place in a vaguely defined future, as America follows Europe and the world down the long, hopeless path toward socialism. The three classmates, then the woman, and finally the steel king join forces with hundreds of other intelligent, freedom-loving industrial leaders and workers to halt and reverse the slide. They do this by going on strike, by withdrawing their services, by shrugging and walking away from duty, as Atlas might have done had he grown tired of holding up the world without reward.

Henry Rearden has invented a new form of metal, stronger and more durable than any before it, yet he is despised and ridiculed for his efforts by the wife, mother, and brother he supports. He falls in love with rail heiress Dagny Taggart, sister of the ineffectual head of the Taggart empire, James Taggart. Hank and Dagny know upon first seeing each other that they are like-minded people. "We haven't any spiritual goals or qualities," Hank tells Dagny with pride. "All we're after is material things. That's all we care for." For that reason, "it's we who move the world and it's we who'll pull it through."[25] A mission, still somewhat nebulous, is accepted.

Dagny wears a bracelet made of Rearden Metal, although other women think it fit only to make rails. To her it represents the beauty of Hank's intellectual power and his drive for money. Rearden continues to play the game, providing metal for a flagging economy, holding up the world, until he is told by Dagny's childhood friend Francisco d'Anconia that it is time for him to shrug and walk away from a system that takes without giving in return. When Rearden refuses, he takes a lesser role in the story, and as time passes a lesser role in Dagny's love life. He begins as the novel's Howard Roark, to the point of being taken to trial for not sharing the new metal's formula with other industrialists "for the common good," a trial in which he will not speak up for himself; but as the story progresses it becomes ever more the story of John Galt, whose intelligence if not his integrity is above that of Hank Rearden. For her part, Dagny recognizes her common spirit with at least three of the heroes and shares their beds, as she has the perfect right to do in Rand's system of ethics.

The second male figure in the story, who seems to have been the first to discover a common spirit with Dagny, is Francisco d'Anconia, heir to the world's largest copper-producing corporation. The descendant of a Spanish immigrant who came to Argentina without a dime and became eventually one of the world's richest men, Francisco was educated in the United States and grew up with the Taggart children. As the story unfolds, it becomes clear that Francisco, the man of rational self-interest, had formulated the plan, after the example of John Galt, for the intellectual and industrial elite to "walk away" from all responsibility, to declare a moratorium on brains. Yet when he first appears in the story he is a globe-hopping playboy in search of parties, wasting his own fortune on pleasure and his company's fortune on lavish investments that are doomed to fail. This is, however, a cover for his plot to save the economy by destroying it.

He explains at the appropriate time, to Rearden and Dagny, that he is pretending to be a profligate in order to draw attention away from his plan to take gifted men out of industry in order to destroy socialism. "You can't have your cake," he says, "and let your neighbor eat it, too" (*AS*, 499). He hints that the man who inspired the plan, who inspired all the Atlases to shrug, is the technological genius John Galt. Galt one day broke his chains and withdrew from the corrupt system that could not appreciate and would not reward him; and Francisco realized that this was the answer—for his fellow Atlases, for America, for the world.

D'Anconia and Rearden remind readers of Wynand and Roark of *The Fountainhead* in their mutual love for the same woman and attraction for each other. Rand later explained that like-minded individualists always recognize and love each other. In the case of members of the same sex, recognition leads to fast friendship; in the case of men and women, it leads to sexual love. She refused to consider the problem of jealousy, insisting that men and women of reason always see that it is best for one to win and one to lose.

Ragnar Danneskjöld, another of Rand's noble Vikings, was also a classmate of Galt and D'Anconia and gave up a promising career as a professor to become a pirate. This man, like Leo Kovalensky in *We the Living,* resembles a pagan god and specializes, like Jules Verne's Captain Nemo, in sinking ships—the difference being that he sinks the ones carrying humanitarian aid and raw materials to socialist countries, not those carrying instruments of war. Halfway through the novel he emerges from his mysterious ocean void to explain that he is a Robin Hood in reverse. He is another man of self-interest who has joined the grand scheme to bring collectivist society to its knees and make the world safe for capitalism.

John Galt, the inspiration behind the scheme, is a mechanical genius who once invented a new, more efficient engine for the Twentieth Century Motor Corporation just before the company adopted a policy of paying each worker not according to his ability but according to his need. Galt instinctively rejected this injustice and one day walked away, taking his engine plan with him. He literally stopped Twentieth Century's engine, and the company collapsed. Soon other like-minded young people disappeared, and other companies collapsed. It was then that Francisco hatched his plot and started forming his alliance of Atlases.

For two-thirds of the novel John Galt remains a shadowy figure, almost mythical, haunting the various places where his chosen object of worship, Dagny Taggart, lives and works, aware but unresponsive to the fact that she is desperately searching for the inventor of the new motor. Because of his example of shrugging and walking away from the injustice of collectivist socialism, however, anyone who wants to express puzzlement or frustration at the sad state of the world simply asks. "Who is John Galt?" His name is a household word, yet no one knows or is willing to tell where he is. Dagny finds him only when he wants to be found, and his hiding place is of ultimate importance to the future of mankind.

Dagny Taggart, Rand's greatest heroine, and her brother James form one of the most interesting contrasts in literature. Dagny is masculine, James effeminate. Dagny runs her part of the Taggart line according to capitalist principles, while James joins every state plan to avoid competition. Dagny is a complete individualist, while James is instinctively collectivist. Dagny loves Francisco, Rearden, and Galt, while James makes love but is unable to love anyone. Dagny's affairs are all violent, based not on self-sacrifice but on self-fulfillment, while James's are all merely selfish. Dagny's first encounter with Galt, in a New York City tunnel, is as deliciously violent as that between Roark and Dominique at the quarry farm, and she loves it. Sex for James is a chore.

As her rail line sinks under the weight of her brother's ill-advised policies, as her most efficient workers disappear to join Galt, Dagny hires a plane to follow the latest runaway and ends up crashing in Colorado. When she regains consciousness, she is told that she has made it to "Mulligan's Valley" or "Galt's Gulch," where a colony of great minds waits to return and rebuild the world their strike is helping bring to a mercifully rapid demise. This is Ayn Rand's Utopia of Greed, where gold is the only medium of exchange, the dollar mark the symbol of orthodox economic policy, and everyone who joins the community and its conspiracy takes the oath:

> I swear by my life and my love of it that I
> Will never live for the sake of another
> Man, nor ask another man to live for mine. (*AS*, 731)

Dagny soon learns the ways of this capitalist Shangri-la, and she respects and admires their plan, but she decides at last that she can still save the world by returning to it.

Things grow worse with each passing day, as Rand's story grows ever more strange. Rearden is attacked by socialists in his crumbling factory and is whisked away to Utopia by Francisco, who has been watching over his much-admired rival for Dagny's hand. John Galt at last comes out of hiding, delivers a three-hour (sixty-page) radio address outlining his and Ayn Rand's philosophy of Objectivism, and is captured by state police. He is told that he must either become Economic Dictator of America or be summarily executed. When he refuses to give aid and comfort to the enemies of freedom, he is strapped to a torture machine.

Dagny, Francisco, Rearden, and Ragnar, brandishing guns, rush in just in the nick of time to free Galt; and the great company, at last united, leave in a plane for Colorado. There they wait, living in pure capitalist simplicity, listening to Richard Halley perform his latest compositions at the piano, until page 1168, when the American and world economies finally collapse. Then says the intrepid Galt: "The road is cleared. We are going back to the world." With a flourish this modern savior raises his hand and makes the sign of the dollar in the cool, clear Colorado air (*AS*, 1168).

Atlas Shrugged is a difficult novel to classify. It is both philosophy and fiction. It is both satire and deadly serious commentary. If it is meant to be a love story, it follows none of the usual patterns of spiritual attraction and self-sacrifice, none of the pain and tragedy, none of the fulfillment of other love stories. As social criticism it indicts but does not recommend, and it fails to create a recognizable world to be improved. As a dystopia it provides bone-chilling descriptions of a world gone wrong; but as a utopia its projections are vague and unlikely. Rand gleefully suffocates hundreds of hated socialists on a train, yet she fails to offer details for the better world waiting to be built when such people are gone.

This is Rand's largest novel, the one that cost her the most time and energy, the one she and her followers considered her best. It has since become the holy text of the Objectivist movement. Whether it eventually takes its place as a classic piece of American fiction or is judged merely a huge burst of ideological wind depends upon the taste of future generations. At this time an outsider looking at her career must choose the latter.

Chapter Three

Ayn Rand as Public Philosopher

Ayn Rand read history at university, and she began her writing career doing fiction and film scenarios. She made her initial impression on the American public through a stage play; and her lasting fame is due to the novels *The Fountainhead* and *Atlas Shrugged.* It is thus intriguing that at age forty she began to see herself as a philosopher, and not just a philosopher of aesthetics or of personal ethics but of public reality, and that at fifty-two she abandoned fiction altogether to dedicate herself to the proclamation of a philosophy she called Objectivism.

To understand this metamorphosis, however, we need look only at her plays and novels; for she was from the beginning as much a polemicist as an entertainer. Her move from fiction to philosophy was, if not inevitable, then certainly a natural transition. She explained years after its Broadway production that *Night of January 16th* was not just a play about a murder trial; it was a vehicle to teach its characters' "sense of life" to the audience. Her early novels *We the Living* and *Anthem* were the efforts of a writer desperately trying to warn readers about the dangers of collectivist societies. Her first best-seller, *The Fountainhead,* is an allergorical treatise, replete with didactic dialogues and monologues, on the epistemological foundations of integrity. And *Atlas Shrugged,* the last of her novels, the one her disciples would consider her best, is a passionate condemnation of a society run by secondhanders, one that forces heroes to shrug and walk away.

It is not surprising that when she had exhausted her imagination she would turn her attention to writing philosophy. The novelist with a message but no more tales to tell became a nonfiction spokesman for her cause. She would spend her last twenty-five years, her energies if not her creativity still flowing, repeating her message.

Early Warnings

Reader's Digest was the first publication to credit Rand with philosophic insight and to grant her space to expound it. In 1944, the year following the appearance of *The Fountainhead, Reader's Digest* printed a Rand article entitled "The Only Path to Tomorrow." World War II was still unresolved; and the editors apparently wanted serious writers to offer directions concerning a still uncertain future.

Although the book she was said to be writing for Bobbs-Merrill, with a working title "The Moral Basis of Individualism," was never published, the *Reader's Digest* article reads like the musings of someone with philosophic ambitions. Rand had obviously given a great deal of thought to the philosophic implications of her fiction. Her mind was clearly focused on the themes she would so fervently pursue in *Atlas Shrugged,* published thirteen years later, and the ones she would expound in essays the rest of her life.

One of these themes, even at a time when the United States and the Soviet Union were comrades in arms, was her denunciation of all types of collectivism. Her persistent emphasis on this theme had doubtless cost her publishing contracts in the 1930s; and it would not be popular in this country until the late 1940s; but Rand seemed not to mind being out of step with the times. Collectivism, she told *Reader's Digest* readers, is always totalitarianism; and "horrors which no man would consider for his own selfish sake are perpetuated with a clear conscience by 'altruists' who justify themselves by— the common good."[1] She warned Americans who wished to see a bright tomorrow to oppose all attempts by collectivists to diminish individual rights. She was speaking not of Nazism, the enemy, but of communism, the supposed friend.

She also revealed in this article, for the first time, her vision of the eternal struggle between Active and Passive Man. Active Man, like her Howard Roark and the "Atlases" she would create, needs independence in order to create and produce, the two most important drives of his life. Passive Man, like Peter Keating of *The Fountainhead* and James Taggart of *Atlas Shrugged,* needs collectivism because, being uncreative and unproductive, he must depend upon centralized governmental protection. Any society based on satisfying the needs of Passive Man will destroy Active Man and will itself become uncreative and unproductive. The path to a creative, productive tomorrow for America, as for the world, is the way of individual freedom, a society in which Active Man can achieve his potential.[2] *Atlas Shrugged,* it is obvious, had been conceived. It would simply have a long gestation.

For the fourteen years between *The Fountainhead* and *Atlas Shrugged,* Rand worked as a screenwriter for Hal Wallis Studios, wrote and helped produce the screen version of *The Fountainhead,* and after eight years in California returned in 1951 to New York in order to work full-time on what she believed would be her masterpiece. Perhaps the most significant event during this period was her meeting Nathaniel Branden, a university student with a winning smile and high ambitions. Branden would over the next eighteen years stroke Rand's ego, convince her that she should expand her role as philosopher, organize a band of disciples, and establish the machinery to disseminate the Objectivist philosophy that Rand would formulate in articles and public addresses.

During the years 1944 to 1957, except for an appearance before the House Un-American Activities Committee in 1947 and the obligatory appearances at the time her film was released in 1949, certainly in the years after she returned to New York, Rand was a virtual recluse. She chose not to follow the usual lecture circuit of successful novelists until she finished *Atlas Shrugged* and turned to philosophy; and she disliked parties. Her only real social outlet in those years were informal, irregular "seminars" with Branden's group, which she called "the children" and "the class of '43" for the year *The Fountainhead* was published. This period produced an 1,168-page novel, a conviction that she was meant to be a philosopher, and perhaps the mental aberrations that even her followers would later recognize.

Rand's career as a philosopher began as she wrote *Atlas Shrugged.* It appears that as she wrote, rewrote, and condensed to 30,000 words John Galt's radio address, she found that she had the message and the mind and therefore the duty to provide a philosophic platform for a generation of "new intellectuals." Galt's speech contains all the elements of Objectivism. The world is facing a time of moral crisis. The choice is freedom or collectivism. New intellectuals must volunteer to live the rational life. They must subscribe to the principles that *A* is *A,* that existence exists, and that man is capable of perceiving ultimate reality.

Galt says that each person must earn his own way, accepting nothing more or less than the rewards of his own labor; that he must drop all dependence on mysticism, all belief in God, all tendency to sacrifice himself for others; and that he must avoid all collective morality, thought, and life. He must be Randian Man. Galt explains that the sorry state of contemporary society is the direct result of modern man's irrationality, altruism, and collectivism. Heroic individualists have been cut down to the size of dwarves; looters have confiscated the achievements of productive men; and mysticism hurries us all toward a new dark age. Modern society can be saved only when men take the Objectivist Oath, the one taken by the men of Galt's Gulch.

Atlas Shrugged made quite a splash. It was reviewed and either praised or damned as much for its philosophic as for its literary merits and demerits. From the late 1950s through the 1960s and into the mid 1970s, Rand was much in demand as a public speaker and for interviews. She published and edited her own journal and turned collections of articles and speeches into best-selling paperback books. She became one of America's most honored and reviled thinkers and came to think of herself as the most creative and profound philosopher of her time.

Public acclaim came as swiftly after the publication of *Atlas Shrugged* as it had come slowly before *The Fountainhead*. Soon after its appearance she was interviewed by CBS correspondent Mike Wallace, and the script of the interview was widely published in newspapers and magazines. *Commonweal* reproduced sections of it, parts relating to religion, in order to support an earlier negative review of *Atlas Shrugged*. Was hers really a philosophy of selfishness? "Selfish? Most certainly," Rand assured Wallace. "Every man has the right to exist for himself—and not to sacrifice himself for others." Was she anti-Christian? "I am not merely anti-Christian—I am anti-mystical. The cross is the symbol of torture, of the sacrifice of the ideal to the non-ideal. I prefer the dollar sign—the symbol of free trade, therefore of the free mind." Did she consider herself the most creative thinker alive? "If anyone can pick a rational flaw in my philosophy, I will be delighted to acknowledge him and I will learn something from him. Until then—I am."[3]

Rand was questioned again and again about some of the things she said in that interview. She later denied, in an interview with Edwin Newman, ever saying such things about the cross; yet she reaffirmed the same idea in slightly different terminology; and she defended and expanded upon the virtue of selfishness and continued to challenge anyone to find flaws in her reasoning. Since to her mind no one was ever able to do so, she died with complete confidence in her own infallibility.

She announced soon after the publication of *Atlas Shrugged* that her next book would deal with epistemology, the philosophy of knowledge, which she rightly called the basis of any systematic philosophy. This was probably the book *Reader's Digest* reported she was writing in 1944. The book, except in introductory form, was never written. Nor was a book, except for scattered collections, written on the other branches of philosophy. Rand never became a systematic philosopher, leaving it to readers to make systematic sense of her hundreds of articles and public addresses.

She either never found the time or simply did not have the gift to become what tradition identifies as a philosopher. Yet her passionate indictments of modern society, her stream of public addresses and articles on philosophic themes, the impact she had on modern thought, the intellectual legacy she left the world—all these things qualify her to be what we might call a public philosopher. She dealt with philosophic issues. She devised and propounded a unique set of principles by which life should be lived. She enjoyed perhaps the largest and most loyal following of any living philosopher of the modern Western world.

The New Intellectual

Rand's debut as a public philosopher was the publication in 1961 of her book *For the New Intellectual: The Philosophy of Ayn Rand.* She dedicated this book to "those who wish to assume the responsibility of becoming the new intellectuals." This was merely a preliminary credo, she made clear, for the developed epistemology based on the radio address of John Galt.

For the New Intellectual was composed of one sixty-five-page essay, the title piece, the only new material; brief selections from *We the Living* and *Anthem;* twenty-five pages from *The Fountainhead* ("The Nature of the Second-hander," "The Soul of a Collectivist," and "The Soul of an Individualist"); and a lengthy 138 pages from *Atlas Shrugged* ("The Meaning of Money," "The Martyrdom of the Industrialists," "The Moral Meaning of Capitalism," "The Meaning of Sex," "From Each According to His Ability, to Each According to His Need," "The Forgotten Men of Socialized Medicine," "The

Nature of an Artist," and "This is John Galt Speaking"). From her choice of passages it is easy to see that she is drawing her philosophic themes from her fiction. Her novels and to a lesser degree her plays will be the new Torah, while the essays to come will be the Commentary.

The long opening essay is worth studying in detail. It represents Rand's first step from fiction to public philosophy, and like most of her steps it is not tentative. She introduces it with a preface, a frank look at herself, that seeks to explain why she is switching to a new form of expression. She asks herself whether she is a novelist or a philosopher, and answers that she considers herself both, as should any true novelist, for one cannot paint a true picture of human existence without using a philosophic framework. The choice, she says, is not between having and not having a framework but between making it explicit or implicit. Beyond that choice lies a second, more decisive one: whether to project a philosophy that is already in existence—a borrowed one—or to create one's own. She says that she decided to make her message explicit; and as to borrowing or creating her own: "I did the second."[4] Rand has never been subtle, secretive, or derivative; and she will not start now.

Rand had formulated and refined this essay, her "maiden" philosophic address, in speeches given between 1959 and 1961 at a number of college campuses. There she had spoken of the cult of altruism sucking the lifeblood from America; the satanic influence of Immanuel Kant, the man she blamed for destroying the achievements of the Renaissance; and the positive moral benefits of capitalism.[5] Those speeches, usually titled "Faith and Force: The Destroyers of the Modern World," solidify into the keynote address for her philosophic career.

She opens with the assertion that America's cultural bankruptcy, its decline in morality, results from its new sense of life: a feeling that the human mind is impotent, that it cannot know ultimate reality, and that reason is no better than mysticism. This sad state of affairs is due in large part to the fact that intellectuals have forsaken their guardposts and permitted mystics to infiltrate our city, spreading lies.

She argues that the professional intellectual and the professional businessman should be brothers, both having been born of the industrial revolution, both the sons of capitalism. They once worked arm in arm to supplant the rulers of the dark ages, the businessman replacing the king, whom Rand calls "Attila," the intellectual replacing the mystic, whom she calls "the Witch Doctor." Attila and the Witch Doctor both hated reason because it threatened their power and joined forces in the dark ages to subdue rational individualism. Attila used a club, the Witch Doctor superstition.

It was the Renaissance, when Aquinas rediscovered Aristotle, that ended the reign of the Witch Doctor, freeing man from bondage to faith; and it was the industrial revolution, produced by man's liberated mind, that ended the tyranny of Attila. The first nation built by the new breed of men, the producers, was the United States. The founding fathers were both intellectuals and businessmen, some of them both at once, and they knew that there is no antipathy between these brothers. Rand concludes: *"Intellectual* freedom cannot exist without *political* freedom; political freedom cannot exist without *economic* freedom; *a free mind and a free market are corollaries"* (*FN, 23*). The reason early American society attained all three freedoms and established the corollary was that intellectuals and businessmen allied themselves against dictatorship and mysticism.

The golden age was, however, tragically brief. While the American businessman continued to do his job, continued to be productive and to provide prosperity for all, the intellectual defaulted. He had supplanted but had not effectively challenged the assumptions of Witch Doctor morality. He refused to bury the Witch Doctor's fatal ethic of self-sacrifice, medieval altruism, and moral cannibalism. Regression set in with René Descartes, who openly doubted the certainly of the external world and urged dependence on one's own consciousness. It continued with David Hume, who said that philosophy is merely a game, since man's conceptual faculties are as limited as his physical skills. It reached its nadir with Immanuel Kant, who with his critique of reason returned philosophy to the level of mysticism and legitimatized the old altruistic morality. Kant led directly to Hegel and Hegel to Marx, who denied both mind and soul and said that only matter exists.

Rand says that the intellectual's job should have been to give the businessman a rational base for operation. He was to think while his brother acted, just as the businessman was to act upon the thought of the intellectual. But in his new, self-imposed bondage to mysticism all the intellectual could give the businessman was pragmatism, a new form of Attilaism. The truth is what works, he told his brother; but under pragmatism there is seldom either truth or work. Even the so-called advocates of capitalism, Bentham and Spencer, failed to create "a rational society with a code of rational morality" (FN, 40). While Bentham hobbled capitalism with the obligation to provide the greatest happiness to the greatest number of people, Spencer made the moral justification for capitalism the survival of the human race and stressed the superiority of cooperation to individualism. It was perfectly predictable that someone like Karl Marx would translate this altruism into communist humanism and reenslave half the world's population.

Not only did the intellectual fail to provide a philosophic base on which the businessman could stand; he actually came to view the businessman as his enemy, as the Attila the businessman actually replaced. He portrayed his brother not as a producer but as a looter. He could not believe that his wealth resulted from effort, labor, productivity, and began to shout "Robber!" At the same time, he came to see himself as the protector of the poor from the rich; and he left the businessman, the bad guy of his scenario, to fend for himself. Since the businessman was never supposed to formulate philosophy, when left to his own devices he deteriorated intellectually. He not only became an anti-intellectual Babbitt, but also began accepting governmental subsidies and handouts and depending on the cooperative programs of a collectivist society. While the intellectual called the businessman immoral and the businessman called the intellectual impractical, in fact the businessman became impractical and the intellectual immoral.

Rand ends this intriguing and creative if a bit fantastic scheme of history by calling for the rise of a new intellectual. He would be guided by reason and reason alone, value his own individual self above all else, and never surrender his mind to mystics or brutes. As if summoning patriots to the defense of their country, she asks rugged individualists long silenced by oppressive majority opinion to step forward and be counted, to make restitution for the failure of past intellectuals, to seek reconciliation with businessmen. The new intellectual will supply capitalism with a firm ethical foundation, teaching men that it is the most practical and moral system on earth. She ends passionately: "The intellectuals are dead—long live the intellectuals!" (FN, 67).

The Virtue of Selfishness

For the New Intellectual, which followed *Atlas Shrugged,* was widely read and reviewed; and much of the commentary was hostile. Critics found her advocacy of selfishness, her enthusiasm for raw capitalism, her rejection of all nonrational assumptions altogether unacceptable. Yet it was obvious that she had a gift for striking nerves, that she knew how to gain attention, that she had made her point. People who had ridiculed and ignored her fiction took her philosophy seriously. Rand was hooked. Essays were easier and quicker to write and disseminate than fiction; and they were a more direct route to public awareness than novels. They would be her vehicle.

As a forum for these essays, Rand decided in 1961 to publish a journal dedicated to the propagation of Objectivism. She and Branden would copublish and coedit, Rand doing most of the writing and Branden running the shop. The journal, which was called the *Objectivist Newsletter,* first appeared in January 1962 and ran under this name and later under the names the *Objectivist* and finally the *Ayn Rand Letter* through January 1976. It occupied her time, absorbed her remarkable energy, and spread her thought across the country and the world for fourteen years. Its addresses and essays were from time to time collected into paperback books. She wrote no more fiction; she was now a philosopher. Sales from the two big novels made her financially secure enough to devote all her time to the really important things of life.

As she was beginning this new phrase of her career, *Mademoiselle* introduced Rand to its readers as part of its series on contemporary "Disturbers of the Peace." She seemed pleased to be considered a disturber and set out to prove it. She was not a conservative, she began, because conservatives link capitalism and mysticism, while she rejected all religion and considered herself "a radical for capitalism." Capitalism should never apologize for its history, she went on, for it was the government-created monopolies of the nineteenth century, not capitalism, that were responsible for the economic excesses recorded in history books. "Second-handers," advocates of a mixed socialist-capitalist economy, sought and won government subsidies and franchises and subverted the true course of capitalism. She went on to advocate a complete separation of economics and the state. The capitalist, working for money and even more for the love of production, working in a free market, could restore the American spirit.

She moved from economics to answer questions with grand assurance on aesthetics. Art, including literature, should be judged by the image of man it projects. Good art portrays man as strong, competent, able to find happiness in this world through heroic effort. Bad art and literature, which she would not tolerate in a world of her making, portrays man as weak, ineffective, and at the mercy of internal and external forces of degeneration. The writers she admired? Victor Hugo, despite his socialism, because of the heroes he created; Dostoyevski, despite his mysticism, because of his firm moralism; and Mickey Spillane, writer of detective stories, because for him all human acts were black and white. She found Mike Hammer, Spillane's moral avenger, a thrilling figure. In contrast, there was Tolstoy, the writer she disliked most, and his *Anna Karenina,* the novel in all of literature she considered the most vile.[6]

The years 1962–65 were heady ones for Rand and the Objectivist movement. The Nathaniel Branden Institute, busy spreading her message, grew by leaps and bounds. Rand was reviewed and covered by a number of national magazines. Subscriptions to the *Objectivist Newletter* grew steadily. She was being taken seriously as a philosopher. In 1964 she published a lecture on ethics and thirteen of her articles plus five by Branden from the *Newsletter* as a new book, *The Virtue of Selfishness,* subtitled "A New Concept of Egoism." She guessed rightly that this provocative title would sell books.

She admits in the book's introduction that she is using the word *selfishness* because it provokes controversy—but that it provokes simply because people are afraid to grant it legitimacy. Selfishness is merely "concern for one's own interests," and nothing is more natural. The reason people think of it as evil is that "altruists" have made men slaves to self-scrificial duty, the most unnatural characteristic of man. Altruists, she says, cannot tolerate man as self-respecting and self-supporting; their minds are too limited to imagine simple "benevolent co-existence" among self-sufficient men. She insists that she is out to create an altogether new ethic, one based on rational self-interest, "the values required for man's survival *qua* man," for true human survival.[7]

The lecture that opens and sets the tone for this collection had been delivered at a University of Wisconsin symposium on "Ethics in Our Time" held in February 1961. It shows that Rand was already wrestling with the problem of how modern ethics missed its mark and how Objectivism could return it to the straight and narrow pathway. She says here that the mystics of the past who based ethics on the arbitrary "will of God" have been replaced by "neomystics" who base ethics on "the good of society," which she labels "a whim." Objectivism, on the contrary, bases ethics on the Aristotelian principle that the primary goal of each organism is the maintenance of its own life, or self-interest. Objectivism can save modern man from the "altruists" who would make him a self-sacrificing "smoo" happily offering himself as a meal for every undeserving neighbor (*V*, 14–33).

During the next two years Rand was drawn increasingly to questions of man as a political and social being; for three of the articles in this book deal with government and human rights. An article called "Man's Rights," first published in 1963, asserts that only a free, capitalist society, built on individual rights, can hold the respect and support of its citizens. There is, she explains, only one human right, the right to life, and one corollary to it, the right to private property, which enables a person to produce something useful to himself and thus enjoy life. The best government is one that provides these and only these two rights.

The opposite of a free society, what she calls a "statist" system, has dominated man down through history: democratic Athens, imperial Rome, monarchial France, gas-chamber Nazi Germany, slaughterhouse Soviet Russia. All such systems, democracies, monarchies, dictatorships, have tried to guarantee every right but the human ones, the rights to life and property, just as American Democrats were doing in the 1960s. It is always the "violator of man's rights" who calls for states to guarantee a job, a home, a decent standard of living. A "collective right" is no right at all. Collective rights sacrifice individual freedom for the common good (*V*, 92–109).

The greater part of these essays first appeared in the *Newsletter* under the section called "Intellectual Ammunition Department," where Rand answered questions sent in by readers. The impression given is that her thought was molded by the give-and-take of intellectual confrontation; yet it is only too obvious that these questions are too soft, that they come not from challengers but from disciples, that they simply provide Rand with opportunities to expound theories already neatly packaged. They are the "straw men" her critics accused her of setting up against her fictional heroes, easily reduced to impotence by the sweeping Randian sword.

One question reads: What does the person who is motivated and guided by rational self-interest do in emergencies, when he must decide whether to endanger his own safety to help someone else? Rand answers that it is entirely reasonable to help another person, even a stranger, if one is asked to do so and if doing so does not threaten one's own life or limb. It is rational to risk one's life for a person one would not want to live without. But she warns not to go out looking for needy people to help; and she says without equivocation that the rational person will not feel responsible for ending the poverty or ignorance of people outside his field of self-interest (V, 43–49). In an essay later in her career, she explained that Archibald Ogden, the editor who risked his job at Bobbs-Merrill to see that *The Fountainhead* was published, was in fact looking out for his own self-interest, making sure that he was given credit for publishing a work of true genius.

Another question: What happens when two men of rational self-interest find that they have a conflict of interest? The answer is that there can never be a conflict of interest between rational men. Qualifying this statement by saying that only free men in a free society—which of course we do not have today—can think and live in a completely rational manner, she sets down specific principles by which rational men, even in this imperfect world, may avoid conflict (V, 50–56). Still her answer, though logical if one can believe in objective, rationally derived truth, is entirely unsatisfactory; and it indicates a severe weakness in Rand's Objectivism. Two men who want the same job or the same contract might well work out a logical solution as to which one wants it and deserves it more; but the mere finding of a logical solution does not guarantee that the emotional conflict between them will be resolved. It is more likely that there will be warfare or that one of them will have to adopt behavior Rand condemned as self-sacrificial.

Another question: Doesn't life at times require some compromise on the part of rational men? Rand's answer: Decidedly not! Compromise always means doing what one knows is evil, and for an Objectivist there "can be no compromise on moral principles." There can be adaptation to unpleasant circumstances, such as working for an employer whose sense of life you do not share, but only if you pretend to share that sense of life is there compromise. There can be no compromise between a property owner and a burglar, between freedom and statism, truth and falsehood, reason and mysticism, life and death. Every issue is black and white. To perceive moral grayness is to compromise with evil (*V,* 68–70, 75–79). Rand's own refusal to compromise made her a strong evangelist for Objectivism; but in time it left her a bitter old woman. Without such radical definitions of truth there could have been no Objectivist movement.

Still another question: How can a person lead a rational life in an irrational society? Having called American society irrational and having admitted that only in a rational society can a person live a rational life, Rand performed some interesting verbal and logical gymnastics answering this one. In fact, she begs the question in grand style by merely handing out a principle of life for this society: "One must never fail to pronounce moral judgment." There is no greater evil, she writes, than moral agnosticism. She challenges the "mystical" adage "Judge not that you be not judged," calling this an abdication of moral responsibility, "a moral blank check." She offers instead: "Judge, and be prepared to be judged." The person who lives according to objective reality must speak up and condemn wrong if and when silence sanctions evil (*V,* 71–73). Rand did precisely this, time and again.

Question: Should Objectivists oppose public projects that help the needy? Answer: Oppose every one because any collective program, no matter how well-motivated, robs individuals of personal freedom. To adopt the maxim "I am my brother's keeper" is to make his misfortune my mortgage. Even "humane" programs like providing medical care for the aged is a collectivist trap that enslaves doctors and forbids them the freedom of trading their skills for the highest offer. Medicare is for Rand equivalent to saying that society should permit a young hoodlum to rob a bank because he does not have a yacht, a penthouse, and a supply of champagne. It is wrong to establish collectivist programs to clean up slums, plan new cities, educate the masses, or even liberate poor artists from poverty. Each such program strips individuals of liberty. They are the moral equivalent of cutting out one man's eye and giving it to a blind man because those in power think it a good idea that everyone see (*V,* 80–85).

The early 1960s were a time of racial unrest, and Rand dedicated several articles to racism. Her position, as usual, failed to please either liberals or conservatives; and it certainly did not satisfy advocates of black progress. She condemns racism as the most basic, primitive, barnyard variety of collectivism. She denies that there is such a thing as racial achievements or failures; and she says that only a capitalist system, in which each person is treated as an individual and not as a member of a race, can liberate men from racist thinking. She condemns equally the Southern politicians who make laws to keep blacks in their place and the federal government that enlarges its powers so as to see that blacks are given greater opportunity. She condemns equally the conservatives who deny black progress and the liberals who fictionalize it. She is equally opposed to segregation and busing to achieve racial balance (V, 126–34). This immigrant woman with no black friends seemed unable to grasp the enormity and complexity of the racial issue.

She concludes *The Virtue of Selfishness* with an article called "The Argument from Intimidation," which clearly shows her frustration with trying to teach Objectivism to a society not yet ready for it. She describes the way professors in university classrooms across the nation teach moral uncertainty to our future leaders. Their premises: only the stupid fail to appreciate modern art and literature; only the ignorant continue to believe in pure reason; only reactionaries support capitalism; and only warmongers speak out against the United Nations. These enemies of truth are themselves the products of a morally bankrupt system, and they in turn pass their bankruptcy on to future generations (V, 139–43). There is a tense, defensive determination in Rand's words, the kind of determination born of numerous battles on college campuses. She will not surrender to the collectivists. Objectivism will one day be taught to young Americans. A revolution is on its way, and its leader is ready.

The Playboy Interview

Late in 1963 and early in 1964, as Lyndon Johnson secured his hold on the electorate, Alvin Toffler of *Playboy* came to interview the rising new star of the radical right. The interview, a carefully pruned edition of several hours of conversation, appeared in the March 1964 issue of the popular "girly" magazine, which has so consistently sought legitimacy through its intellectual offerings. Rand's followers considered the interview important enough to have it reprinted, and it is available from the Palo Alto Book Service.

In his introduction Toffler says he found this "intense, angry young woman of 58" an outsider to both the literary and philosophic establishments yet a best-seller in both fields and *sui generis,* one of a kind. He was obviously impressed from the start by this chain-smoking woman whose opinions were set in chunks of pure granite.

It is a wide-ranging conversation. Rand tells Toffler that the chief tenet of Objectivism is that "objective reality exists independent of any perceiver or any perceiver's emotions, feelings, wishes, hopes or fears." Objectivist ethics hold that "man exists for his own sake, that the pursuit of his own happiness is his highest moral purpose, that he must not sacrifice himself to others, nor sacrifice others to himself." "Productive work" is the chief goal of all her Objectivist followers; and she aggressively argues that it is that and that alone which gives them happiness—and anyone who places other people above his own creative work is an "emotional parasite."

When asked her opinion of the feminist movement, she says, as she will not say some years later when feminism has moved to a higher level of demand, that "what is proper for a man is proper for a woman." She urges that "woman can choose their work according to their own purpose and premises in the same manner as men do."[8] She does not foresee what she will later call the "sex war" about to be declared. She will tell Edwin Newman only a few years later that women who want to be equal or superior to men go against woman's true nature, which is to look up to man.

She is asked about romantic love, and once again she speaks her mind. The only person capable of true romantic love is one driven by passion for his work; for "love is an expression of self-esteem," which means that it is essentially selfish. To love is to consider another person important to oneself. Love is not self-sacrifice. The greatest compliment is to say, "I need you." As for pleasure, it is a secondary consideration, a by-product of the happiness that comes from being close to someone who fulfills one's needs. She concludes that man must use reason, not be driven by biological drives, in order to determine how best to use the sexual machinery handed him by natural history.

When asked "Is Objectivism dogmatic?" Rand answers dogmatically that it most certainly is not. According to her definition, a dogma is something accepted on faith, and Objectivism depends purely on reason. She denies ever having called the cross a symbol of torture, although she undoubtedly had done so, but admits believing that it symbolizes the sacrifice of a good man for bad ones, an idea obviously repugnant to her. In the name of that event, she explains, men have been taught to sacrifice themselves for their inferiors, and "that is torture." She tells Toffler that she would personally die for Objectivism, but more important, she says she would live for it, which is something far more difficult.

When asked her opinion of contemporary literature, she answers, "Philosophically, immoral. Aesthetically, it bores me to death." She hastens to explain that she finds it devoted primarily to depravity and that after a short time nothing is as boring as depravity. Again as in previous statements, she names Victor Hugo and Mickey Spillane as her two favorite authors. What makes them great, she says, is that their primary purpose in writing fiction is to project the image of the ideal man "as he might and ought to be."

Turning to politics, she says that the only proper function of government is the "protection of individual rights," that both taxes and military service should be entirely voluntary, and that the draft is unconstitutional since it is a form of involuntary servitude. She favors an economic boycott of Cuba, withdrawal of the United States from the United Nations, and severing diplomatic relations with the Soviet Union. She says she considers Richard Nixon nothing more than a me-too-er, but she is excited about the candidacy of Barry Goldwater. Once again she feels obliged to point out that she is not a conservative, for conservatives compromise capitalism by mixing it with moderate social welfare. She is a radical for capitalism.

She takes pains to criticize William F. Buckley's "conservative" magazine *National Review,* which had run an unfavorable Whittaker Chambers review of *Atlas Shrugged,* for its drive to mix capitalism with mysticism. She scorches John Birchers for spending more time opposing communism than defending capitalism. And she ends by castigating all the political groups currently passing through the American scene and forswearing any personal ambition to run for office. There is not a political mainstream in the America of 1964, she says; there is not even a stream, there is only a stagnant swamp.

The Unknown Ideal of Capitalism

Rand's coolness toward politics began to warm as the year's election campaign progressed and she saw more of Barry Goldwater. In his steel-gray hair, jutting jaw, and Arizona tan she saw the personification of her literary heroes Howard Roark and Hank Rearden. In an interview with *Look* editors for an article on "Goldwater People," she publicly endorsed Goldwater, the first time she had made an endorsement since 1940, the first time since she was important enough to matter. She said that she would vote for him because he believed in the rights of individuals. She admitted that he was not the advocate of pure capitalism she really wanted; but she called him the best candidate for president in fifty years, presumably going back to William Howard Taft for her last hero.[9] She was said by those close to her to have been sorely disappointed when Goldwater went down to defeat at the hands of Democrat Lyndon Johnson, a supporter of social welfare.

At the end of 1965 the *Objectivist Newsletter* became simply the *Objectivist*. Rand and Branden were still copublishers and coeditors, still in charge of operations, still the major contributors; but the newer, slicker magazine format indicates that the Objectivist movement was making steady progress in both popular and financial support. It was spreading out from New York to other cities and receiving attention on college campuses. Rand did not demur when someone suggested to her at this time that only the Vatican, the Kremlin, and the Empire State Building (where the new *Objectivist* offices were located) knew the real issues of the day. She and her movement were indeed riding high in the saddle. The period from 1962 to 1968, especially the latter four years, would one day be seen as the heyday of Objectivism and of Ayn Rand's fame as a public philosopher.

Late in 1966 there appeared a second collection of Rand's public addresses (mostly given at the Ford Hall Forum in Boston and the Nathaniel Branden Institute in New York) and articles (mostly from the *Ojectivist Newsletter* and the *Objectivist*) called *Capitalism: The Unknown Ideal*. Rand herself contributed eighteen of the twenty-four chapters, with two by Branden, three by Alan Greenspan (then an economic consultant, president of his own firm of Townsend-Greenspan and Company), and one by Robert Hessen (a doctoral student in history at Columbia University and now with the Hoover Institute in California).

The book is dedicated to the memory of that brief shining moment, Rand's Camelot, when America came close to establishing a true capitalist society. Had she known his work, she might have paraphrased G. K. Chesterton's comment that Christianity (capitalism) has not failed, it has not been tried. Despite it tremendous potential for good, despite the fact that even in its impure form it once brought prosperity and progress to this land, it is still unknown by most Americans. With this book, however, they will no longer be ignorant of or have an excuse for neglecting "the only system geared to the life of a rational being."[10]

She defines capitalism as the only social system based on the recognition of human rights, particularly property rights, without governmental interference with the means of production. She credits a group of manufacturers in seventeenth-century France with the best early description of such free enterprise. Louis XIV's finance minister Colbert asked these men what the government could do to help them, and they replied, *Laissez-nous faire,* just leave us alone (*C,* 140). This spirit, transplanted to the new world, helped create the freest society ever known to man. It produced an independent population of small manufacturers who in the nineteenth century gave America the highest standard of living on earth. The great period of world peace between 1815 and 1914, she says, can be attributed to the strength of capitalism in the Western world; and she argues that under capitalism both Europe and America abolished manual servitude and achieved the highest level of equality in history.

This golden age now lies in scattered remnants, tragically mixed with altruistic socialism. It was ended in part because intellectuals failed to provide it with a moral base on which to launch new initiatives and partly because second-rate industrialists preferred government grants and favors to making their own way. These so-called businessmen, choosing socialist security over individualist opportunity, cut the legs off giants like James J. Hill, Cornelius Vanderbilt, Andrew Carnegie, and J. P. Morgan, the self-made men who had earned their fortunes by effort and ability. Time after time the government granted monopolies to beggars, breaking the backs of competitive producers; and when the system began to fail through inefficiency, the victim was blamed for the crime.

Rand had set much of her novel *Atlas Shrugged* along Dagny Taggart's railroad, and she was particularly interested in the way capitalism's enemies had brought down the great rail empires. The worst cases were Hill's Great Northern, which grew to greatness without government help and was then prosecuted as a monopoly, and Vanderbilt's New York Central, which he had to save from the state's attempt to destroy him through legal piracy (*C,* 102–8).

Rand says that such men should have been left alone to make as much money as they could, to grow as strong as their abilities permitted, with the nation the beneficiary.

These great men were not left alone. They were in fact hobbled beyond recovery by an ever-expanding body of government regulations and were blamed for the failure of the "mixed" economy that brought them down. Rand calls the businessman "the symbol of a free society—the symbol of America"; but she acknowledges that to most Americans, especially those who fear the challenge of individualism, the businessman is regarded as little better than a criminal who requires laws to control his appetites, who is required to pay for the errors of others, and who is penalized for his virtues. He is, in her words, "America's persecuted minority" (*C*, 44).

She blames the conspiracy to destroy the great capitalists on a "tribal" instinct. Critics of capitalism have always said they were acting against individualism for some mystical notion of the "common good" or the "public interest," both of which are rooted in the primitive tribal notion that individuals must curtail their personal drives and conform to the standards of the clan. This tribal instinct not only has limited the talents of rugged individualists, but also brought on warfare between classes and even nations. Modern world conflict, Rand says, is rooted in the tribal notion of nationalism and would gradually disappear in a world of individualists (*C*, 35–40).

It is therefore with a measure of glee that Rand announces the failure of the American socialist consensus. Government by consensus, the policy of the 1960s, means no ideology, no morality, no policy, with all decisions of state being made in accord with the wishes of the mediocre middle majority. This system, which despises and ruins its Howard Roarks and Hank Reardens, is by 1966 beginning to collapse, because it has no philosophic foundation. The Vietnam War has created such confusion, with fuzzy goals and shifting policies, that society is stumbling toward a fall. Students with no moral ground on which to walk are rebelling against the system that failed to nourish them, yet they have nothing constructive to offer in place of the establishment they hope to bring to its knees. Mario Savio of the Berkeley Free Speech Movement, Rand says, is Immanuel Kant's true son (*C*, 214–46). Out of the ruins to come, she hopes, will emerge a new golden age of Objectivist-inspired capitalism.

Objectivist Epistemology

In 1967 Rand published still another collection of essays from the *Objectivist,* all of them related to the subject of epistemology, all originally published between July 1966 and February 1967, entitled *Introduction to Objectivist Epistemology.* This thin volume represented her first and only concerted attempt to begin a systematic presentaton of Objectivism. She called it a "preview of my future book," perhaps a first chapter, since modern philosophers consider epistemology the first item on their agenda.

She begins by saying that epistemology, the definition of universal concepts, is the central issue of philosophy and therefore her first concern. She summarizes the four schools of philosophy from which one may choose his epistemology: extreme realism as represented by Plato, who considered universals real entities but also said they exist independently of concrete phenomena; moderate realism as represented by Aristotle, who considered universals real but held that they exist only in concrete phenomena; nominalism, which calls them merely names; and conceptualism, which says they exist only as images in the mind of man. Rand explains that Objectivism accepts Aristotle's moderate realism, teaching that the senses are valid transmitters of reality to the brain, that "existence exists" objectively, that *"A is A."* Since a society's fate depends upon its epistemology, on how it views universals and reality, America must learn Objectivism or be lost in confusion.[11]

Objectivism says universal concepts are neither revealed by a supernatural mind nor invented by the mind of man but are "produced by man's consciousness in accordance with the facts of reality." Recognition and description are the work of man, the rational creature, working according to the dictates of objective reality (*I*, 71). The solution to every human problem is accessible to the man who lets his reason probe the parameters of objective reality. His only pitfalls along the way are his own irrational nature, which is untrustworthy, and the answers of mystics, who enslave reason and block visions of reality.

This book, in the form of a series of essays, is Rand's first attempt at presenting her systematic philosophy. It shows her to be a more disciplined thinker than her free-wheeling articles, essays, and addresses had heretofore indicated. Had she continued in this vein, had she written other books as concise as this one, books on ethics, aesthetics, logic, she might have established herself as a systematic philosopher. Such books never came; and judging from the style of this one—its obtuseness, its deficiency in the kind of energy found in her "occasional" writings—it is perhaps just as well.

A Romantic Manifesto

If Rand readers expected her next book, published in 1971 under the title *The Romantic Manifesto,* to be a second volume in her systematic philosophy, they were disappointed. It is more likely that they were happy to see her return to her old form. This new book, which does deal with aesthetics, is composed of articles written between 1962 and 1971, with a concluding short story written in 1940. It is the first book Rand published after her separation from her disciple Branden, the first not to include at least one of his articles. By 1971 he was persona non grata, and in fact after the 1968 schism Rand added a postscript to each new printing of the books that still featured his writings: "Nathaniel Branden is no longer associated with me, with my philosophy or with the *Objectivist* (formerly the *Objectivist Newsletter*)."

The loss of Branden is not evident in this book because the articles here are for the most part from the period prior to the separation; but there does seem, in the articles written after 1968, a diminution of powers. The *Objectivist* continued to be published for two and one-half years before being replaced by the *Ayn Rand Letter,* a less ambitious project. She continued for a time to make public addresses and turn out articles, and they provided fodder for other books; but there was no further attempt at systematization, fewer collections, less talk of turning America from its errors. Rand's voice grew more shrill, her personality more negative, her denunciation of morals more bitter. Her growl became a snarl.

Yet *The Romantic Manifesto* (the title a conscious challenge to Marx) is for the most part a preschism work, featuring only two pieces written and published after Branden left. It is on the whole a fiery, aggressive, challenging book, the last of its kind. It represents the essence, though in scattered form, of Objectivist aesthetics, following in a line the earlier collections on self-interest, capitalism, and epistemology. Since it deals with the arts and literature, it is perhaps Rand's most revealing work.

The preface sounds a pessimistic tone. "There is no Romantic

movement today," she says, although she considers herself still a
romantic. As a movement it has been destroyed by its own repre-
sentatives, by exponents who failed to see what they had in their
very hands. But the old Rand fire is not dead. If there is to be a
romantic movement in the future, she hastens to say as if there will
be one, "this book will have helped it to come into being.[12] It is
obvious that she considers herself the bridge linking the Camelot
of romanticism (roughly analogous in time, spirit, and theory to
the Camelot of capitalism) to the future of Objectivist romanticism.
There is still hope, she says, even if at the moment it is precious
and waning.

For Rand the essence of romanticism is its recognition of man's
faculty of volition; and this is what sets it off so distinctly from the
naturalism that followed it and now holds center stage in American
letters. She explains here that romanticism was born in the late
eighteenth century because this was a time when an Aristotelian
sense of life validated the power of human reason and a capitalist
economy freed man's mind to translate ideas into practice. Romanticism was a movement that could have given the world a grand
new era of progress, teaching individualism and moral values, providing capitalism with the philosophic and aesthetic foundation for
even greater achievements in the future.

Sadly, this did not happen. As a brilliant, sometimes quite violent
adolescent—who died young—the romantic movement failed to
translate its sense of life into philosophy and burned itself out,
choking on its own energy. Since it was by nature a rebel against
the establishment, and since that establishment happened to be
classicism, romanticism felt obliged to despise classicism's emphasis
on reason and wickedly espoused the cause of emotions. While the
romantics fought for a heroic vision of man, they surrendered their
best weapon, reason, to the enemy. They defended instinct, condemned industrialism, admired mysticism, despised capitalism, rejected reality, and so weakened by altruistic morality they easily
fell prey to naturalism (R, 103–20).

Rand either did not understand or was unwilling to admit the
complex nature of romanticism, and chose to emphasize one of its
tenets and ignore the others. She considered herself its sole legitimate
descendant, with the possible exception of Mickey Spillane. She
believed that she alone among modern writers consistently followed
the romantic conviction, learned from Aristotle, that while history

describes things as they are, fiction must describe them as they might and ought to be. She says that it took 2,300 years for man to discover the medium, the novel, with which to convey Aristotle's vision of fiction; and she seems to feel that it took romanticism another hundred years to produce an Ayn Rand, who would put the novel to Aristotelian use.

She blames the resurgence of mysticism and its denial of reason for romanticism's early demise. Before the nineteenth century, she argues, literature had made man the victim of outside forces, of some tragic inner flaw, or of a capricious God, all three being forms of mysticism. Only romanticism, with its emphasis on free will, broke this chain and liberated the hero. As romanticism committed suicide, that old sense of helplessness came pouring back to condemn man once again to tragedy. The naturalist school that appeared in the mid-nineteenth century portrayed man once again incapable of individuality, happiness, or even virtue. Zola, Balzac, and Tolstoy wrote of perverts, addicts, and psychotics. While romanticism had created characters larger than life, naturalism made them smaller. Literature became pessimistic, art primitive, and music as irrational as the jungle (*R,* 123–28).

Contemporary readers are made so skeptical of heroism, she says, that they cannot abide heroes. Because heroes threaten the pessimistic vision of life, they must be held up to ridicule. She points to the way filmmakers felt they had to re-create novelist Ian Fleming's James Bond. In the original novels Bond was a romantic hero, but in the films he is ridiculous, a caricature of himself, grossly exaggerated, the butt of tongue-in-cheek parodies. Such naturalist enemies of romanticism call romantic novels "thrillers" and brand them simplistic, unrealistic, and escapist. Rand advocates a repeal of the "Joyce-Kafka amendment" to literature, which "prohibits the sale and drinking of clean water, unless denatured by humor, while unconscionable rot-gut is being sold and drunk at every bookstore counter (*R,* 133–41).

Moving to another metaphor, Rand says that in order to rediscover the statues of Greek gods beneath the rubble of naturalism, we should dust off our Victor Hugo. In her introduction to a new edition of Hugo's *Ninety-Three,* included in this volume, she calls him the world's greatest novelist, a man who obeyed the Aristotelian command to portray a race of giants, men as they can and ought to be. Let critics call his characters unrealistic, their language the-

atrical, their stories escapist, Hugo is still the best antidote to
collectivist anthropology our bankrupt society can hope to find (*R*,
153–56). She notes that when she reads Tolstoy she feels she is
walking in an unsanitary backyard; when Dostoyevski, in a chamber
of horrors; when Mickey Spillane, in a park with a military band
playing; but when Victor Hugo, in a cathedral (*R*, 43). An interesting metaphor, this, from someone who despised religion; but it
made her point.

For Rand art, which includes literature, is "the indispensable
medium for the communication of a moral ideal." It can be seen as
the voice of the artist's sense of life. The mighty legions of scoffers
arrayed against romanticism should not at all deter the Objectivist
from his assigned mission: to make heroes that will demonstrate
man's true nature; to project "the ideal man," the man guided by
rational self-interest, man as "an end in himself" (*R*, 162).

The Anti-Industrial Revolution

The year 1968 was crucial for Rand. Her loss of Nathaniel Branden, though other disciples stepped into his shoes, left her without
her major inspiration. She continued to write, to pronounce keen
judgments on contemporary society, to appeal for a return to reason;
but after the schism she seemed deficient in energy—and what is
worse, in solutions. A few of her later analyses of events are incisive,
but they are more negative than positive, more destructive than
constructive.

A second book of collected articles and lectures to appear in 1971
was *The New Left: The Anti-Industrial Revolution,* which dealt with
American education and the anti-intellectual biases that have formed
it. The pieces in this book, unlike those in *The Romantic Manifesto,*
were written in 1969 and 1970, in the period just after her break
with Branden. It is interesting to note the difference in tone of the
two collections; and it is equally interesting to read in Rand's introduction the reason she chose to publish these shrill proclamations.
She says that she received a letter from a young graduate student
at Northern Illinois University, one G.M.B., asking her to make
available in a convenient form her recent articles and addresses on
education and the challenge college students were making to the
American system. Was this young person a new inspiration, a re-
placement for the Nathaniel Branden she had lost? Possibly. There

is no evidence that he ever visited Rand or that there was involvement beyond the initial correspondence; but once more she found in a new disciple, perhaps representing a whole generation of new disciples, a reason to collect and publish.

The articles and addresses G.M.B. was asking her to publish in book form, all written and given in 1969 and 1970, dealt with the student revolution; and she says in the introduction that *The New Left* is intended for college students and those who care about them. Her basic argument, no surprise to anyone who knows her thought, is that the student unrest of the day is due to the fact that students have not been taught to think rationally. She says that American colleges are filled with weak administrators, skeptical professors, and ignorant students, all inhabiting a Kantian world of antirational and therefore anti-industrial prejudice. Students are rebelling against this dead-end street they are forced to walk, yet their protests are as unfocused as their brains.[13]

Rand applauds the students for rejecting the type of education they have been forced to swallow; but she mourns the fact that they also are rejecting the only positive accomplishment of their fathers: modern technology. She contrasts what she calls the marvelous human achievement of the Apollo mission to the moon with what she calls the human degradation of the Woodstock rock festival, which she labels a tribute to Dionysus. She explains that while Apollo demonstrated what the brotherhood of rational men can accomplish, Woodstock proved what can happen when men revert to tribal mysticism with its jungle beat. "It is man's irrational emotions that bring him down to the mud," she writes in the summer of 1969, the summer of Apollo and Woodstock, "it is man's reason that lifts him to the stars" (*N*, 57–81).

Everywhere she looks she sees evidence of a new anti-industrial conspiracy among the young. The ecology movement to save the environment is to her part of an anti-intellectual, anti-rational, anti-industrial movement that dances to the rhythm of African drums. "Anyone over 30 years of age today," she says, "give a silent 'Thank you' to the nearest, grimiest, sootiest smokestack you can find," for smokestacks are a symbol of capitalism. This misguided younger generation is out to destroy industry and capitalism, the economic hope of the world. She ridicules "Earth Day" as a time when "young people who did not take the trouble to wash their own bodies, went out to clean the streets of New York" (*N*, 127–51).

Behind all of this anti-industrial protest, she says, is envy, the leitmotiv of our age. There is hatred not of vice but of virtue, not of weakness but of strength, not of evil but of good. Critics of progress try to hide their true colors by claiming that they want to make all men equal, when in reality they create ever greater inequality by retarding the capitalism that makes men equal. She goes on in this shrill tone to condemn American women, the most privileged on earth, who protest their condition. They are simply man haters, as the protestors of industry are simply progress haters. Even worse than the women are the men who support their protests (N, 152–86). Everywhere she looks she sees envy.

But she saves her most vicious words for a blistering attack on the American educational system. She takes her text from Victor Hugo's story "The Man Who Laughs." It is about a society that kept children in oddly shaped pots until they were so monstrously stunted and deformed that they could be used to entertain dignitaries. Rand charges that the same process is being carried out against American minds in "progressive" nursery schools, where the emphasis is on conformity and socialization, never on conceptual skills. In such an environment, created by John Dewey, where children are considered too young to learn concepts and are taught only to play fairly, it is only the "maladjusted" and the "misfit" who has any hope of retaining his integrity and going on to be a rational human being.

The damage continues to be done in the higher grades, where knowledge is given out in snatches, and in college, where students are taught that the human mind is incapable of knowing anything for certain. The "comprachicos" of Hugo's story, though physically stunted, still have clear minds and can track down and punish their tormentors in time, while young Americans are so intellectually mutilated that they are incapable of identification and revenge. But in case some of the misfits can be provoked to vengeance, Rand goes on to identify the tormentors for them. The real monsters are not the students, and the mutilators are not capitalists, as their professors say. The culprits are actually the Kantian professors who train teachers to suppress individuality in children, who demonstrate by their own lives that knowledge is beyond the grasp of the human mind.

And so Rand, who begins her book on student unrest by condemning rebellious kids, calling them a Dionysian rabble, concludes by saying that in their capacity to rebel lies America's hope. "You have nothing to lose but your anxiety," she says as she calls them to arms. "You have your mind to win" (N, 187–239). This strange twist is easier to understand if one remembers that one man's terrorist is another man's freedom fighter. Rand approved actions aimed at accomplishing her own goals while condemning the same actions when they supported the goals of her opponents.

Who Needs Philosophy?

So ended the books Rand published during her lifetime. She continued to write articles for the journal, which from mid-1971 to early 1976 was called the *Ayn Rand Letter*. She continued to give occasional lectures and interviews. In 1972 she caused a small flurry of interest by denouncing Democratic presidential candidate George McGovern. She spent 1974 rediscovering and losing again a sister from the past; and in 1975 she suffered an illness that caused her to abandon her writing and close down the *Letter*. In 1979 Frank O'Connor, her husband of just fifty years, died; she survived him by less than three years. The last ten of her seventy-seven years were not happy ones.

Still there remained fire in the ashes. The *Letter* articles, the best of which were published in the posthumous *Philosophy: Who Needs It?*, show a keen interest in contemporary issues, if a somewhat diminished intellectual energy to challenge them, well into the mid-1970s. The attack on McGovern proves that as late as 1972 she was still the Ayn Rand of old. That same year she was asked by *Saturday Review* to add her views to a symposium of such well-known public figures as Ralph Nader, Herbert Stein, Al Capp, and Michael Harrington on the subject "Do Our Tax Laws Need a Shake-Up?" She used the opportunity to go right for the throat of the decent but awkward Democrat's platform. Entitling her response "McGovern Is the First to Offer a Full-Fledged Statism to the American People," she says that Richard Nixon can not be trusted to save the nation but that McGovern can certainly be trusted to destroy it. Her major complaint against McGovern is that he proposes to establish a claim to the total national income. To speak of redistributing the wealth presupposes governmental ownership of wealth, and state ownership of property always crushes a society's producers. McGovern would revive the old leftist slogan and policy: "Who does not toil, shall eat those who do." She says he is more a fascist than a communist, for while communism forbids men to earn for themselves while at least promising to provide for their needs, fascism forces them to earn and then turn their earnings over to the government.[14]

Sensible readers doubtless considered Rand's indictment of the soft, humanitarian politician unnecessarily harsh; and the spirit of the attack is reminiscent of the Ayn Rand who gleefully killed off "second-handers" on her fictional trains. We see more of this spirit in the *Letter,* where an aging Rand refights old battles and fences with new books and even news items. Here she seems more interested in blocking deviation from her dogmas than in blazing new trails. The fire that produced her novels and philosophic essays burns lower but still burns brightly.

She complains that the press praises "consensus" and damns "polarization," when the former is bad and the latter good. She ridicules Nixon's trip to China, calling it morally confusing and politically embarrassing, saying that while America was once a stern Uncle Sam, a fearless cowboy, a dignified Indian, a self-made businessman, it is now merely an international social worker. She reluctantly supports Nixon for president in 1972; but when he falls from grace she sniffs that his pragmatism led to Watergate. She apologizes for agreeing with liberal Supreme Court justices who voted to legalize abortion and restrict artistic censorship. The abortion issue and his religiosity separate her from Ronald Reagan.

As family problems and illness took their toll, Rand fell woefully behind in writing her *Letter;* and in 1975 she at last decided to discontinue publication. At the end she lists evidence that Objectivism is the philosophic wave of the future. She is being quoted regularly by President Ford. The new leader of the British Conservative party, Margaret Thatcher, is a loyal and devoted fan, as are Australian Prime Minister Malcolm Fraser and opposition leaders in socialist Denmark and Norway. In 1974 Rand had written, "I did not want, intend or expect to be the only defender of man's rights, in the country of man's rights. But if I am, I am."[15] Now she felt less lonely.

When she died in 1982, Rand was preparing the collection of articles that would be published later that year by her literary executor Leonard Peikoff under the title *Philosophy: Who Needs It?* While this book was billed as volume 1 of a new Ayn Rand Library series, it lacks the strength to launch any significant project. Composed of a speech delivered at the United States Military Academy in 1974 and scattered articles from the *Letter* (1971–75), it offers little that is new. She goads Boris Spasky in an open letter. She spars with the latest "anti-concepts." She praises the play *The Miracle Worker,* and she condemns B. F. Skinner's *Beyond Freedom and Dignity.*

Finally, as a last will and testament, she calls on Americans to relearn individualism, admiration for productivity, and rational self-interest: the true American sense of life. She tells them to repeal the welfare state as they once repealed Prohibition, that other mistake. She warns them to put altruism in its place, by striking its twin roots of irrationalism and mysticism, before it destroys the home of the free.[16] Thus ended the philosophic musings of Ayn Rand, dedicated defender of individualism, articulate evangelist for the hero, remarkable woman.

Chapter Four

The Themes and Theories of Ayn Rand

From the time *Atlas Shrugged* appeared in 1957 until the day she died in 1982, Ayn Rand returned again and again, in articles and public addresses, to the radio speech of that novel's mechanical genius John Galt. She considered it the essential statement of her public philosophy; and she quoted it as though Galt were a living authority and his words holy writ. She said that in its 35,000 word text, which required two full years to write and condense, lay all the themes and theories of Objectivism. All her later books were merely exegesis.

Galt's message to the American people was a call for each man to earn his own keep, take responsibility for his own but for no one else's life, and be a rationalist, an individualist, a producer. He warned that man's most dangerous enemy, as he works to establish his way in this world, as he becomes self-sufficient, is the temptation to irrational thought, collectivist morality, altruistic ethics, and mystical metaphysics (*AS,* 1009–69). In essence, as Rand had said in *We the Living,* "Man is a word that has no plural" (*W,* 229). John Galt delineated the implications of that principle; and in doing so he said all Rand wanted said.

Objectivism

As her fame grew, as she moved from novelist to philosopher, however, Rand realized that she must develop in greater detail, explain more explicitly, fill in the gaps of John Galt's message. This required another twenty years and another six books to complete, and it established Ayn Rand as a public philosopher.

She called her philosophy Objectivism. The term comes from what she considered the central theme of her thought: that universal concepts or ideas, the ancient problem for philosophers, have an objective reality. She told Alvin Toffler in the *Playboy* interview that "objective reality exists independently of any perceiver or of the perceiver's emotions, feelings, wishes, hopes or fears."[1] And in her definitive statement on the foundations of Objectivism, *Introduction to Objectivist Epistemology*, she explained that her school and hers alone in modern times considered universal concepts to be neither received by mystical revelation nor invented by the mind of man.

Yet she also believed, and made the second theme of her philosophy, that man's mind is capable of perceiving and interpreting these universal concepts. She said that she and she alone followed in direct line from Aristotle, the father of reason, through Aquinas, the father of early modern rationalism, to the twentieth century. She took great pride in being the only true rationalist of her times; and she argued that man is perfectly capable of integrating "the facts of reality" and creating a rational philosophy of life according to a "cognitive method of classification whose process must be performed by man, but whose content is dictated by reality" (*I*, 71).

It requires a careful reading of Rand's novels and essays, followed by studied organization of their detail, to identify and clarify the implications she drew from this basic assumption about reality; but when this is done, Objectivism stands as a distinct and logically coherent if still controversial philosophy. For Rand the external world exists independently of man and man's consciousness; yet man, gifted with superior reason, is capable of understanding, interpreting, and using this reality. Man perceives objective reality through his senses, and his reason integrates it for productive utility. Reason is his only means of true knowledge and his only means of survival in this world. It must therefore be cultivated, protected, and used to the fullest extent of its capacity.

Rand believed that man's rational interpretation of reality would invariably lead him to an ethic of rational self-interest. She said that "man exists for his own sake," that "the pursuit of his own happiness is his highest moral purpose," and that he should not "sacrifice himself to others, nor sacrifice others to himself."[2] The rational man does not borrow the values of others, nor does he impose his values on anyone else, particularly by physical force. He knows that the politicoeconomic system that offers him the best chance to realize his potential is laissez-faire capitalism.

William O'Neill, who has studied Rand's philosophy in a more systematic way than perhaps any other scholar, has summed up the basic principles of Objectivism under the following categories: Rand's metaphysics is objective reality; her epistemology is reason; her ethics is self-interest; and her politics is radical capitalism.[3] This chapter will investigate in some detail these and other themes and theories of Objectivism. My aim is to identify and interpret and evaluate them as "objectively" as possible.

Rationalism

Ayn Rand made clear in her *Introduction to Objectivist Epistemology* that she considered herself an Aristotelian, or a "moderate realist." She rejected the "extreme realism" of Plato, who she said believed in a reality separate from concrete matter and thus accessible to man only through mysticism. She also rejected the postclassical schools of nominalism and conceptualism, both of which she said denied the objective reality of concepts (*I*, 2). For Rand concepts are objectively real and are bonded to the concrete world. They are readily accessible to man through his reason. Complementary to her emphasis on the objective nature of reality, then, is her emphasis on the rational nature of man. No image of man that neglects or denies his rational nature is acceptable to Objectivism.

Rand once said that on her tombstone she wanted one word, the word that best described her philosophy, her sense of life. It was not "Novelist" or "Objectivist" or even "Individualist" but "Rationalist."[4] The heroes of her novels and the object of her praise in philosophic essays are first and foremost men of reason. They do not depend for their knowledge, ethics, or morality upon social norms or mystical revelations. They are coldly rational, self-sufficient, and unapologetic for being what they are. Her most succinct statement of this rationalism appeared in the September 1971 edition of the *Objectivist* when she explained: "I am not *primarily* an advocate of capitalism, but of egoism; and I am not primarily an advocate of egoism, but of reason" (*P*, vii). For Rand reason stands as the foundation of all human achievement. It fosters egoistic individualism, which fosters productivity, which creates and sustains capitalism, which blesses all men. The man of reason reaches to the stars, while the man without reason descends to the mud and chokes on his own irrationality.

As we have seen, Rand credited Aristotle with establishing the value of rationalism; and she said that only in times when Aristotle is the guiding light is man self-confident and productive. When he is not, man is mired in fear and stagnation. One of her most intriguing metaphors for rationality and irrationality is found in her essay "Apollo and Dionysius." There she compares the Apollo 11 moon shot to the Woodstock rock festival, both coming in the sultry summer of 1969. That man is capable, simultaneously, of such noble scientific achievement and of wallowing in field mud to the beat of jungle drums demonstrated to her man's vital choice in life. He may choose to follow his rational nature and climb to the stars through technology, or he may choose to follow his irrational urgings and sink to the earth in a drunken, mystical stupor. The choice is Apollo, god of light, or Dionysius, god of wine (*N,* 57–81).

In all of Rand's writings, both fiction and philosophy, the theme of rationalism is closely linked with that of individualism. The man of reason is always an individualist, shunning society's values, following only the urgings of his own mind. Her heroes are strong rather than merciful, resolute rather then considerate. Their most outstanding, decisive, unalterable characteristic is supreme egoism.

In the novella *Anthem,* the myth of one man's escape from collectivist totalitarianism, she said that Ego is the one word that such a regime must strike from man's vocabulary in order to enslave him. The hero of *The Fountainhead,* Howard Roark, destroys his own building rather than see it modified by lesser minds; and in court he defends his actions with an appeal to individualism. John Galt, Francisco D'Anconia, and Ragnor Danneskjold in *Atlas Shrugged* are willing to bring the world's shaky economy to the ground to satisfy their own egos. Throughout her career Rand praised such individualists, men who go their own way, taking pleasure in lives independent of the herd.

Self-Interest

The rational individual, the man of ego, is by nature a selfish being, a man of supreme self-confidence and self-interest. Ayn Rand called such a man a hero, a person to be respected and praised for his human spirit. It grieved her that selfishness had a negative connotation, and she blamed this on the advocates of what she considered destructive altruism. When broadcaster Mike Wallace asked her if hers were a philosophy of selfishness, she answered vigorously: "Selfish? Most certainly. Every man has a right to exist for himself—and not to sacrifice himself for others."[5]

This was the interview in which she declared that she was not only anti-Christian but altogether antimystical, by which she meant that she opposed all religion. She explained that the central symbol of Christianity, the cross, represents and advocates the sacrifice of a good man to bad man and that rational self-interest forbids this kind of tragedy. The individualist may find it hard at times to swim against the current of collectivism, but he can always find a few like-minded friends who will help him, and in time his selfishness will be vindicated. Selfishness will not go unrewarded.

It is indeed more than a virtue. It is the foundation for a code of ethics that Rand called "the morality of rational self-interest" (C, 150). The selfish person, she said, is concerned only with his own productive labor, which he does proudly and efficiently, and he does not interfere with the work of others, either to assist or to hinder. This is why men of reason, men of self-interest, will not have conflicts of interest (V, 50–56). Men who value their own lives above all other things are society's producers, the "prime movers of mankind," while men who do not value their lives, altruists, are "metaphysical killers" waiting for a chance to be physical ones (W, vi). Hitler and Stalin were for Rand men of low self-esteem who had to compensate by trying to rule other men with iron fists. Capitalists like Cornelius Vanderbilt and James J. Hill, however, were men of rational self-interest and high self-esteem who had no need to rule their fellowmen.

Rand believed that the individualist must above all other things avoid the modern "cult" of altruism. Altruism, as she defined it, means self-sacrifice, self-immolation, self-abnegation, self-denial, and ultimately self-destruction. It is the vampire that sucks the blood from producers. She believed that medieval Christian altruism, which was set aside by the rediscovery of Aristotelian ethics at the beginning of the Renaissance, was revived by the philosopher Immanuel Kant. Kant was a far worse enemy of individualism, of rational self-interest, than Christianity had been because while Christianity advocated love of neighbor without calling for hatred of self, Kant called for both. Kant taught that an action is moral only if performed out of sense of duty with no benefit to the person performing the act. This sense of duty, this altruism, was Rand's main target as she tried to teach the virtue of selfishness (*P*, 60–70).

For her altruism was a primitive phenomenon, a reversion to a tribal ethic. In prehistoric times, she said, it was necessary to band together into tribes, to think of the needs of others, in order for humans to survive as a race. In modern times it is but a "psycho-epistemological" defense against the opportunities of individualism, a protection of lesser men against the growth of individualists.[6] Altruism is used by the modern "mystic-altruistic-collectivist axis" of "second-handers" who cannot thrive in an open society to keep the "man of ability" in his place. This axis has created the present "Age of Envy," in which the good are hated for being good, the strong for being strong, and the producer for being productive (*P*, 102).

All of which explains why Rand chose to call the *Atlas Shrugged* valley in which her men of rational self-interest waited for the collectivist economy to collapse a "Utopia of Greed." There each man traded his skill for payment in pure gold and in turn paid pure gold for the skill of other men. There no one thought more of another than he did of himself. There each man thought and acted for himself and for no one else. Men of undiluted selfishness lived in harmony with each other, without conflict of interest, because all of them followed the dictates of reason. The symbol of their society was the dollar sign. This was utopia for Ayn Rand. She would continue to delineate its principles throughout her life.

The Hero

For Ayn Rand the man of rational self-interest, the man who refused to live for the sake of another man, was a hero. She never seemed to notice or care that critics ridiculed her novels for their outsized characters, too large, too perfect for this world. She glorified in portraying man not as he is but as she supposed he should be. At the end of *Atlas Shrugged*, after her heroes have decided to return and save the world they have brought to its knees, she wrote: "My philosophy, in essence, is the concept of man as a heroic being, with his own happiness as the moral purpose of his life, with pro-ductive achievement as his noblest activity, and reason as his only absolute." And in her introduction to the 1968 edition of *Night of*

January 16th she wrote: "The motive of my writing has always been the presentation of an ideal man."[7]

The first hero Rand encountered as a young woman was the fictional British officer serving the crown in India, the blond soldier Cyrus. In her own writings the early heroic figures were all women—Kira Argounova of *We the Living,* Karen Andre of *Night of January 16th*—and it was not until *Anthem* that she created her first really ideal man. He was Equality 7–2521, later called the Unconquered and later still Prometheus. He was the one who learned to say, despite a totalitarian regime's mind control, "I am a man. This miracle of me is mine to own and keep, and mine to guard, and mine to use, and mine to kneel before!" (*A,* 110). His spirit was in Howard Roark of *The Fountainhead* and in Hank Rearden, Francisco d'Anconia, Ragnor Danneskjold, and John Galt of *Atlas Shrugged.*

The hero is probably Rand's central theme—and theory. She was undaunted by the fact that he does not exist in flesh and blood, that the few times she thought she had found him she was sorely disappointed. She acted as if she believed that by capturing him in fiction she had proved him a universal concept and that since all concepts are potentially concrete he can exist in this world. At the end of *Atlas Shrugged* she wrote: "I trust that no one will tell me that men such as I wrote about don't exist. That this book has been written—and published—is my proof that they do." This is Rand's ontological argument for the existence of heroes. With Anselm of Canterbury, who believed he proved the existence of God this way, she said that since she could conceive of men greater than ordinary men, they must exist. One can recognize them because they have faces that bear no trace of "pain or fear or guilt."

Her hero was the Active Man who needs his independence in order to be creative and productive, his twin passions in life. In the *Playboy* interview she told Toffler that the Active Man's paramount goal in life, to be productive, comes before his friends, his family, even his own well-being. "A man who places others first," she once said, "above his own creative work, is an emotional parasite."[8] The Active Man, the prime mover of society, is at home only on the job, is effective only in a free market, and trusts his own reason over the altruistic plots of collectivists.

It is interesting, given the impact of the figure "Cyrus" on the young Ayn Rand, that none of her heroes is a soldier. Nor does any go to the ends of the earth to do battle with the forces of evil, with the possible exception of the industrialist-intellectual-pirate Ragnor Danneskjold, who uses his naval fire power to sink the ships of altruistic nations sending charity to needy ones. Yet even her Ragnor seems to be waiting for his opportunity to open an automobile factory somewhere in Nebraska. In point of fact, Rand's heroes are all builders of one sort or another, erecting their office buildings, establishing factories, founding banks. They are all in business of one type or another.

Rand once said that her favorite novel among those she did not herself write was *Calumet "K."* In that story, written early in this century, the young hero Bannon struggles against great odds and opposition to build, of all things, a giant grain elevator in the Midwest. Rand admired his "self-confident resourcefulness, his inexhaustible energy, his dedication" to his own personal vision. Her own Howard Roark would build not the public monuments socialism erects with forced labor to the memory of altruists but private buildings dedicated to and paid for by capitalists. Roark's erections are therefore larger, more practical, and more durable than those of collectivists. They are also among Rand's most durable creations.

Her heroes all suffer at the hands of jealous enemies. Roark and Rearden are both thwarted again and again by the machinations of lesser men. Roark loses and is forced to resign a number of commissions because he will not compromise his convictions and conform to popular conventions. Rearden loses trade and ultimately his factory because he insists on following the dictates of his own will. Both men are brought to trial for being individualists, men of rational self-interest. Yet Rand writes stories as they should be, not necessarily as they are in real life, and both of her heroes go free. Roark persuades a jury that he did the right thing when he blew up a housing complex, while Rearden's clear-eyed refusal to answer absurd questions cows his accusers into helpless surrender. Other heroes—D'Anconia, Danneskjold, Galt—also suffer but also win in the final scenes. It would seem then that Leonard Peikoff is right when he argues that at heart Rand was a romantic optimist. After the dark days of the late 1930s, her dark chapters, those in which her heroes suffer, are brief and transitory. Vindication and victory are inevitable and sweet. A benevolent universe favors her type of man. Her good guys always win.

The Villain

If Rand's heroes wear white, her villains are always dressed in black. Her villains, particularly in *The Fountainhead* and *Atlas Shrugged*, after she shed the more complicated characters of earlier works, are as dastardly as her heroes are good and true. Yet hers are a unique kind of villain: men who are evil because they are weak, because they lack moral fortitude, and this because they lack an epistemology capable of creating an ethic of individuality. Without an epistemology, a sense of life's potential, they are without hope.

They compose an interesting gallery, as interesting in fact as that of the Rand heroes. There is, in the early novel *We the Living*, Kira's cousin Victor, who becomes a Party member because the Party is the way up the socioeconomic ladder, who denies his heritage, his family, his own true self in order to reach the top of the dung heap, who sells himself and loses himself for privilege. There is in *The Fountainhead* poor Peter Keating, a man without rational direction, a man who cannot trust his own judgment or his own talent, a true "second-hander" who eventually ends up on the slag heap of architects and human beings. There is Gail Wynand, also of *The Fountainhead*, Rand's only moderately sympathetic—and tragic—villain, who had the makings of a hero, a self-made man who earned a fortune by giving people what they want, but who is eventually destroyed by the same people; in the end he can only provide the money for the real hero, Howard Roark, to erect a building for him.

There is Wesley Mouch of *Atlas Shrugged*, the socialist prime minister of collectivism, the man who longs for cooperation to the point of extinction, who will lead his country down the altruistic road to oblivion. There is James Taggart, also of *Atlas Shrugged*, heir to a rail empire, a man of weak personal identity, who makes bargains with other rail owners to avoid competition, who seeks and lives off government protection and subsidies, who will suck away profits for personal pleasure until the essence of his empire is gone and the shell collapses. And there is Rand's archvillain, the devious, malicious Ellsworth Toohey of *The Fountainhead*, a Rand "looter," a man who wants power not over himself, his work, his destiny, not even over nature or wealth, but over other men.

The key characteristic of Rand's villains is their "secondhandedness." The term *second-hander* was first used by Howard Roark in

The Fountainhead to explain to his friend Gail Wynand, on Wynand's yacht as the two men sailed the high seas, the type of man who hates because he is the exact opposite of the individualist. Second-handers have no personal identity. They try to live other people's lives and let other people live theirs. They seek to be part of a clan, a tribe, a herd, a collective unit of society; and they live only for what they call the common good. Consequently, they make no decision independently of the will of the ignorant majority and are thus no different from other men. Later in the novel, as he defends himself in court for blowing up the housing project he designed, Roark identifies the second-hander this way: "The basic need of the second-hander is to secure his ties with other men in order to be fed. He places relations first. He declares that man exists in order to serve others" (*AS*, 738).

Rand's villain, her second-hander, is Passive Man. He is in essence a parasite who lives off the work of Active Man. So long as society cares for him, he is willing to submit to the tribe and obey the common will. He seeks privileges and encourages others to seek them as well.[9] He lives off the work of others as does any thief or "looter." Yet despite the damage he can do, in the final analysis he is powerless against Active Man. He will always be with us, as cancerous as Ellsworth Toohey, as disgusting as Peter Keating, as tragic as Gail Wynand, but he can never win out over the individualist. Rand paints him in stark colors, and she permits him to exercise temporary malevolent power, but in the end she always has him paint himself into a corner from which he cannot escape. Rand's heroes will prevail—her villains will fail.

Either/Or

Very few of Ayn Rand's characters fall into the gray category between hero and villain. Only in her early fiction did she experiment with complexity. In her best-selling later work all the characters are black or white. Good and bad for her did not relate to conventional moral standards but depended upon a character's sense of life; and her good characters were those who followed rational self-interest, while the bad ones followed the herd.

This penchant for painting in stark colors, for making such dramatic contrasts between good and evil, for creating faultless heroes and irredeemable villains, evoked critical ridicule. Patricia Donegan of *Commonweal,* commenting on *Atlas Shrugged,* chuckled that all her heroes were handsome, clear-eyed, and keenly intellectual, while all her villains had flabby jowls, blood-shot eyes, and muddled brains.[10] As did other critics, she described Rand's characters as mere mannequins used to model Objectivist dogmas.

What critics generally saw as a major literary flaw, her inability or unwillingness to create characters with the mixture of motives to make them human, Rand herself considered her greatest strength. Ethical choices, she said, are always clear-cut, and the people who make them become just as black and white. In the *Playboy* interview she said: "I most emphatically advocate a black-and-white view of the world." "Before you can identify anything as gray, as middle of the road, you have to know what is black and what is white, because gray is a mixture of the two. And when you have established that one alternative is good and the other is evil, there is no justification for the choice of the mixture."[11] She never wavered from this faith. She once said that while her knowledge of facts had increased and her outlook had broadened over the years, her basic assumptions concerning human personality and moral judgments never had.

She spoke out regularly and with force against what she called the "cult of moral grayness," against the tendency to say issues are clouded by complexity, that no position is all right or all wrong. In the June 1964 edition of the *Objectivist Newsletter* she admitted that a person should listen to both sides of an issue before making a judgment about it; but she denied that both sides can have equal claim to the truth. She had always found it rather easy, relying on her reason, using Aristotelian concepts, to separate right from wrong, good from evil, because she knew how to apply universal concepts to specific situations. She said that gray is a compromise with black, indeed in most cases a prelude to black, and only the irrational person or the coward, both second-handers, cannot make a definite choice between good and evil. Did she believe that all issues, like her fictional characters, are either all black or all white? "You're damn right I do," she piped (V, 75–79).

She argued that any compromise with false ideology, any admission of its claim to truth, is like a property owner's compromise with a burglar, freedom's compromise with slavery, life's compromise with death. Compromise is doing what one knows is wrong. There was in her scheme of things no way to do the wrong thing for the right reason or vice versa. "Working for an employer who does not share one's ideas is *not* a compromise," she wrote, "but pretending to share his ideas, *is.*" For Ayn Rand, "There can be no compromise on moral principles" (*V*, 68–70). One can hear a door slamming shut.

Her followers were subject to periodic evaluations of their orthodoxy, and those who had compromised themselves were disciplined or purged. Deviation was compromise with falsehood. One of her former disciples, Jerome Tuccille, tells of purges at the Branden Institute in the mid-1960s that are reminiscent of if not as deadly as the Russian Communist party purges in the mid-1930s.[12] Branden was himself purged in 1968 for what Rand considered ideological and moral compromises, for thinking and living in the gray zone. Branden himself remembers how over the years she grew ever more suspicious of deviation and developed an obsession about loyalty,[13] the logical result of a black-and-white morality.

Capitalism

The whitest of all Rand's whites, the truest of all her truths, the principle least to be compromised, was capitalism. Capitalism was the creation and in turn the creator of heroic individualism. It was, when unspattered by the black ink of governmental controls, the perfect economic and social system, the only one under which an individualist can and will thrive. Rand's watchword was the French merchants' request to Louis XIV's finance minister Colbert, *"Laissez-nous faire"*—the resounding "Leave us alone." She insisted on a separation of economy and the state patterned on the lines of separation of church and state. She insisted, when asked her philosophy of economics, that she was "a radical for capitalism."[14]

For Rand capitalism is the only economic system "geared to the life of a rational being." It is not only history's most practical system but the most moral as well (*C*, vii–viii). Only under the capitalism of the late nineteenth century did men of rational self-interest flourish and produce as men are capable of doing. Only then was true freedom for all achieved. Capitalism wiped away European feudal serfdom in the fifteenth century and American slavery in the nineteenth. For her the industrial American North before 1900 was the most progressive, equitable society of all time, a golden age of economic and political liberty, a Camelot. She loved to contrast it to the feudal South of the same period, where ignorance, poverty, and racism still dominated. Capitalism was the difference (*V*, 129–30).

She was particularly incensed by the shibboleth that the love of money is the root of all evil. She had Francisco d'Anconia of *Atlas Shrugged* insist that "money is the barometer of a society's virtue"; he warns: "Run for your life from any man who tells you that money is evil. That sentence is the leper's bell of an approaching looter"; and concludes: "The man who damns money has obtained it dishonorably; the man who respects it has earned it" (*FN*, 108). It is not the love but the hatred of money that is the root of evil. Hank Rearden, at his trial, says: "I refuse to apologize for my ability—I refuse to apologize for my success—I refuse to apologize for my money" (*AS*, 480). Since money results from success and success from ability, money is the visible symbol of talent. It is a source of pride, not shame, and it is a positive virtue. The paradise of *Atlas Shrugged*, the place where men of rational self-interest prepared to save the world, is called a Utopia of Greed, and its symbol is a gold dollar sign.

Rand had her own version of the history of Western civilization. In it Aristotle and his descendants, men who chose reason over mysticism, freedom's insecurity and opportunity over religious and political controls, led the way toward capitalism and progress. Plato and his descendants, "Attilas" who wanted to control man by force and "Witch Doctors" who wanted to do so by mysticism, held man back from these goals. The Middle Ages were a time of Platonic mysticism, the Renaissance and industrial revolution times of Aristotelian rationalism, when intellectuals and businessmen combined to create a climate for progress. So long as these blood brothers, the thinker and the doer, both sons of reason, were allied, all went well. They helped create what Rand considered the most nearly perfect society in history, the American North in the late nineteenth century.

Sadly, however, while the businessman continued to expand the scope of freedom and prosperity, the intellectual defaulted. Following Immanuel Kant, intellectuals returned to the discredited mysticism of the Middle Ages, questioned the reliability of reason, called the businessman a robber baron, called into question the motives and achievements of capitalism, and left the businessman without the philosophic base he needed to operate successfully. Kant led to Marx and retrogressive socialism, with its altruistic morality and governmental controls. Businessman were stripped of their freedom to operate. They reacted to the intellectuals' neo–Witch Doctor mentality by turning to a neo-Attilan one. The golden age came to a tragic halt, its light scattered about a landscape ravaged by collectivism, with only remnants of its glory to remind men of a better day *(FN, 3–67)*.

Time and again Rand attacked the notion that capitalism dehumanizes workers. Under the great capitalists, men of rational self-interest, workers made more gains than at any other time in history. It was not businessmen but second-handers, looters, who were responsible for the excesses, abuses, and ultimately the decline of capitalism. Capitalism gave the modern world its only period of world peace, from 1815 to 1914, and it helped dissipate the tribal racism that eventually led to the two world wars of the twentieth century. It was not the capitalists but the looters, enemies of capitalism, who stirred up envious men, second-handers, particularly those in the government, to bring the capitalists down to the average level. Government controls, concessions, subsidies all led to a "mixed" economy that rendered the capitalists ineffective. They were taxed, restricted, and publicly shamed until they either gave up and joined the cooperating tribe of second-handers or were crushed by the combined power of Attila and the Witch Doctor. Cornelius Vanderbilt and James J. Hill were Rand's shining examples of capitalist virtue. She was willing to forgive the way they bribed legislators to remove restrictive "artificial" barriers to free trade because the barriers were evil *(C, 102–8)*. Such men carried the gold dollar mark high. They were, in her words, America's persecuted minority.

The good guys of history were the capitalists, the bad guys those jealous second-handers and looters who brought them under control "for the common good." "Businessmen," Rand once mused, "are the symbol of a free society—the symbol of America" *(C, 62)*. They do not exist under dictatorships, either right-wing or left-wing, and they do their most virtuous work in a society that gives them free rein. They are often the scapegoats for the failed policies of lesser men who mix capitalism with socialism and need someone to blame when inevitably their schemes go sour. But Rand argued that capitalists should never be ashamed of doing what they do so well. Money is health, and capitalists bring it to a nation. Without capitalists a new dark age waits to descend.

This is of course the reason Rand believed it so important that America protect the right of private property. While capitalism in this country remains polluted by the socialist policies of recent administrations, America is still the most nearly capitalist nation on earth; and Rand believed that its future depends upon preserving as much of its former capitalist spirit and practice as possible. Private property, she said, is the key to survival. Next to guaranteeing the right to life, the most important function of a government—the second of only two a government can legitimately assume—is to guarantee the right to private property. Man's life is worth living only if he can be productive, and productivity requires private property (V, 94).

Rand saw how difficult the road to a new capitalist era would be for a nation that has strayed from the straight and narrow to dabble in collectivist experimentation. She called the 1960s and 1970s an "age of envy," a time when the individualist was despised for being better than the common man, when the great man was penalized simply for being great.[15] It was a time, she said, when men were hated not for their vices but for their virtues. The much-vaunted "egalitarianism" of the day was actually just a "fig leaf" to cover the jealousy of looters, a device to make all men the same, which meant to make them all equally inferior. The liberation that she heard being preached from every rooftop was to her mind liberation from reality. The equality of income being advocated would result in less equality than ever because competition and productivity and therefore access to goods would inevitably decline (N, 153–82).

As we have seen, Rand believed that the antitechnological mentality of that period was part of an anticapitalist plot to make America a second-rate economy. For her "a *restricted* technology is a contradiction in terms," and when technology declines so does a nation. She saw the ecology movement, the preoccupation with protecting the environment from technology, as the misguided efforts of ignorant youths convinced they were defending nature but in reality serving the interests of envious second-handers and looters who would destroy the free-enterprise system. This assumption led her to make such "Dr. Strangelove" statements as: "Americans over 30 years of age today, give a silent 'Thank you' to the nearest, grimiest, sootiest smoke stacks you can find." The ecology movement, she was sure, was out to destroy the last remnants of capitalism and set up a global dictatorship run by Attilas and Witch Doctors.

Its leaders wanted to destroy the very system that had freed them from slavery, and they were doing it by denouncing capitalism for doing what it was meant to do and did so well—create abundance (*N,* 127–50).

Rand believed that America was nearing the end of its philosophic resources and rapidly approaching moral bankruptcy. Its intellectuals had taught it that man's mind is impotent, reason unreliable, reality unknowable, all of which leads to retrogressive mysticism. She saw no mainstream of philosophic, economic, or political thought, only a dismal swamp. She saw America despised, both by foreign nations and by its own citizens, not because of its flaws, its weaknesses, its failures, but because of its virtues, its achievements, its successes. Yet these very virtues, achievements, and successes proved to her that beneath its mystical, collectivist facade America still retained elements of the capitalism that for one brief shining moment had almost made it as great as it could have been.

These elements, she argued, must be preserved and cultivated. The political leaders she saw around her would never be able to do so, however, and she openly ridiculed them all. She despised all Democrats, the more democratic they were the more she hated them, and with the exception of Barry Goldwater and to a lesser degree Gerald Ford she despised most Republican "me-too-ers" as well, what with their support of a mixed economy and their tendency to mix capitalism with religion. She believed that the future hope of capitalism lay with Objectivists, radicals for capitalism, the new intellectuals who would link arms once again with businessmen and provide capitalism with the philosophic and moral base on which to build and work effectively. Hope might be rather distant, but it was in her vision. It depended not on politicians but on philosophers.

Collectivism

If capitalism was Rand's whitest virtue, collectivism was most surely her blackest vice; and she saw it growing by leaps and bounds both here and abroad. "Politically, the goal of today's dominant trend is statism," she wrote in 1972, using statism as a synonym for collectivism. "Philosophically, the goal is the obliteration of reason; psychologically, it is the erosion of ambition."[16] Collectivism, irrationality, lethargy—these three were always bosom buddies. She had her spokesman for the totaliterian state in *Anthem* explain that in his collectivist system "What is not done collectively cannot be good" (*A*, 81). And in *Atlas Shrugged* she captured the essence of collectivist philosophy in the slogan of the bankrupt Twentieth Century Motor Company: "From Each According To His Ability—To Each According To His Need" (*AS*, 668). This was the company that was forced to close its gates when its mechanical genius John Galt walked away from its altruistic, collectivist statism to form his Utopia of Greed.

By Rand's explicit definition, statist socialist collectivism is the philosophy that makes man both a ward and a servant of society. He exists not for himself but for others (*FN*, 48). It imposes without the consent of the governed the humanitarian projects that should be carried out voluntarily, if at all. It makes, in Rand's memorable phrase, my brother's misfortune my mortgage (*V*, 80–81). It encourages tribal dependency and discourages independent action. Above all, as she made clear in *Anthem*, it forbids men to use "I" and demands the use and even the worship of "We" (*A*, 114).

For these reasons, Rand says, collectivism is not merely impractical and ineffective; it is patently evil. It is the root of war, racism, and slavery. When individualism is denied men, when they are forced into tribal uniformity, the result is armed conflict between tribes, paranoid obsession with preserving our territory from the encroachment of the enemy, and ultimately the attempt to control not just the actions but the thoughts of other tribes. "Men who are free to produce," Rand wrote, "have no incentive to loot" (*C*, 38). The same is true of nations. Horrors and atrocities no man would consider committing for his own sake are readily perpetrated by those who claim to act for "the common good."[17]

Rand never missed a fictional opportunity to blast collectivism. *We the Living* describes the collectivist Soviet state during the early years of the Bolshevik regime as Russians lose their political, economic, and personal freedom. *Anthem* describes a collectivist state of the future in which men have been stripped even of personal identity, all for the sake of "We." *The Fountainhead* describes one man's fight against the collectivist tastes and values of a society afraid to think for itself. *Atlas Shrugged* describes the America that might yet be produced by collectivist economic planners and offers the only alternative Rand saw for men of rational self-interest: to go out on strike. Politically, she said in a *Letter* article, collectivism breeds a swarm of "little Caesars" who strive for power over their fellowmen, while culturally it breeds a "lower species" of "little Neros" who sing depraved odes to altruism while productivity goes up in smoke.[18]

In an intriguing "open letter" to Soviet chess champion Boris Spassky, Rand mused about the way *his* country, a collectivist state, acts in the "sport" of politics. How would he like it if in chess some arbitrary authority continually changed rules? How would he like being required to play with a partner, as a team, without being able to disagree with his partner's decisions? How would he like to play under two sets of rules, one for the proletariat and the other for the bourgeoisie? How would he like having a sudden judicial decree make pawns more valuable than kings? How would he like being told to sacrifice strong pieces for weak ones? How would he like prizes given to losers, while winners are put to shame for being good?[14] All this was to her Soviet collectivism, the purest form of collectivism, the prototype, the exact opposite to capitalist individualism.

Libertarianism

The question of how to classify Rand politically is crucial for understanding her thoughts; yet it is one of the most difficult of questions about her to answer. She voted, when on rare occasion she found a candidate worth voting for, Republican; but Republicans radical enough for her were few and far between. She never found a good word to say for a Democrat. She considered liberals of any sort mere spokesmen for a welfare state in which the major human right was to claim government help for every citizen every moment of the day. She ridiculed conservatives for their tendency to mix capitalism with religion, making it seem an antirational philosophy, denying its basic assumptions and goals.[20] Ronald Reagan, darling of conservatives across the nation and one day to be president, earned her scorn for his views on abortion.

She has been called a libertarian. Many of her disciples did come from one or another strain of that tradition, and many returned to it when they left her. Yet she once told Branden that she hated the word "libertarianism," calling it a misnomer and a confusing term. She was never a member of any party or political movement and felt that her task was only to formulate a philosophic base on which radical capitalists could reestablish a golden age. She had strong political opinions; and it stands to reason that she wanted her ideas put into effect through the political process; yet she established no machinery for that purpose.

Among her "libertarian" themes and theories was the idea that all taxes should be voluntary. She acknowledged that the government needs money to perform the few meager tasks it has the right to perform for its citizens; but she denied that it has the right to confiscate funds for the purpose. She suggested from time to time that revenues be raised through a lottery, which she considered a self-imposed tax that would yield wealth to a few fortunate participants. If further revenues were needed, then citizens should be persuaded with good evidence to give voluntarily.

She considered the military draft of the 1960s unconstitutional, calling it involuntary servitude or slavery. She advocated a volunteer army, which of course came in her lifetime. It is debatable whether the present army is as efficient as a conscripted one. It is certainly contrary to Rand's philosophy that taxes be imposed on the populace to support a collectivist body of mercenaries.[21] To be fair to her, however, what she had in mind was an army of individualists combining forces in moments of national peril as temporary volunteer defenders of freedom. It is no wonder that even the people who shared her libertarian spirit considered Rand naive on this point. It is also no wonder that she gained some uncharacteristic admirers when she opposed the war in Vietnam. To her it was an unjust war because it did not serve America's interests. It was being fought for "altruistic" reasons.

Rand also opposed public ownership of radio frequencies and television channels and said that they should all be sold to the highest bidders and then be classified private property. If the owners failed, they would be sold to more worthy owners, and capitalism would flourish. Yet she was in favor of retaining laws to protect patents and copyrights. They were to her, a writer, the owner of copyrights, the "legal implementation of the base of all property rights: a man's right to the product of his own mind." This is why, she explained, they are always under attack by collectivists, who say that all inventions should serve the common good by being tossed into the common pot (C, 122–33).

Philosophy: Good, Bad, Ugly

Rand blamed the current state of American politics and economics, the loss of individualism and capitalism, on the state of philosophy. She said we act as we do because we think as we do; and she was convinced that America's philosophic poverty stood in the way of its material progress and prosperity.

As we have seen, Rand believed that Aristotle was the greatest of philosophers, the one who showed mankind the truth. The key to his greatness, she thought, was that he trusted man's reason to give him a true picture of reality. Aristotle was lost to medieval Europe, due to the designs of religious mystics who feared him, and the twin oppressors Attila and the Witch Doctor held sway over a dark age. With the recovery of Aristotle by Thomas Aquinas came a Renaissance and the defeat of the Witch Doctor, and following the Renaissance came the industrial revolution and the defeat of Attila. It was at this moment, when men were truly free, that capitalist America was born. The golden age had dawned.

At this moment along came disaster in the person of Immanuel Kant. This German son of a Quietist mother followed in the steps of René Descartes, who had retreated into the Witch Doctor's jungle by questioning the objective reality of the visible world, and of David Hume, who had questioned man's sensual and conceptual faculties; and Kant was to complete this unholy trinity's work of misinformation by calling into question reason itself.

Kant was to Rand the subversive who bored from within to weaken and subvert the cause of reason while as a professor of philosophy, ostensibly an intellectual, claiming to defend it (*P, 64*). She considered him wrong on every major point of his philosophy. Not only did he consider man's mind impotent, saying that it can perceive only phenomenal and not noumenal reality; but he also said that in order to be moral a deed must be performed out of duty, not out of any sense of self-interest. He thus relegated man to the category of servant, enslaving him to mystical authority.[22]

Since Kant's day, Rand said, philosophy has declined precipitously. Nietzsche rejected the Witch Doctor, bully for him, but he elevated Attila to sainthood. Bentham identified capitalism with an oppressive duty to provide happiness to the masses. Spencer claimed that the moral justification for capitalism is the survival of the race and stressed cooperation at the expense of individualism. So the stage was set for Marx to elevate altruism to the level of pseudoscience and enslave half the world's population in a collectivist net. The result is that capitalism and individualism now have no philosophic base from which to operate. It was to provide this base that Rand wrote her novels and essays: to teach the remedial doctrine of Objectivism.

Atheism and Mysticism

Essential to that base, she believed, was atheism. An Objectivist, one dedicated to the restoration of individualism and the reconstruction of capitalism, must above all else not be deceived into believing in God. This of course made her a bedfellow to her despised "altruist" Karl Marx, and strange bedfellows they were, but Rand seemed not to notice or care. It may be that her early atheism resulted from a subconscious admiration for the Marxists who won the Russian soul when she was a girl, that as has been the case with many impressionable young people she incorporated the teachings of her tormentors. This might also explain the admiration she showed in early stories for communists. Whatever the source, she held firmly to her atheism throughout her life; and she believed it just as important to fight the Witch Doctor's mysticism as Atilla's collectivism.

For Rand a mystic was anyone who places another being or cause above man. She said Judeo-Christian mystics forced Aristotle out of Western thought and chained men and their ethics to the arbitrary will of God. With the second coming of Aristotle at the end of the Middle Ages, mystics lost control of man's mind; but through the work of the subversive Immanuel Kant a new type of mysticism rose up to chain men and ethics to what was called the good of society, or the common good (V, 14). Rand spoke out against both kinds of mysticism in the name of man the individual.

Critics have long pondered Rand's antireligious posture. Some have charged that she reflected the typical Russian-Jewish intellectual's contempt for the mystic orthodoxy of the Third Rome, that Objectivism is an American form of anti-Christian Jewish rationalism. One is forced to observe that the composition of her disciples lends credence to this accusation. Yet despite the fact that she sounds more like an alien who does not understand the Western religious tradition than an insider who understands and rejects it, it must be said she is no more anti-Christian than anti-Jewish. She is not the typical anti-Semite some atheistic Jews tend to be, but she certainly has no rapport with her family's religious tradition. Her atheism denies both Jewish and Christian theism. She never spoke of Jews or of Israel or of the holocaust. Religion was to her simply incompatible with self-interest, the keystone of individualism and capitalism, incompatible with Objectivism.

She said that she became an atheist at age thirteen. It was in conversations with her father that she began to see that there was no reason to believe in God, that in fact theism implies the inferiority of man. Leonard Peikoff has noted that as early as 1934, when Rand was twenty-nine, she referred in her journal to religion as the major cause of man's lack of integrity. Already she was identifying religion and communism as brothers under the skin. Communism emerged from the Judeo-Christian tradition and bore striking resemblances to its ancestors; and both subordinated man to a higher power: religion to God, communism to the state. Both listed selflessness, not selfishness, as the highest virtue (*E, 108*).

Rand's atheism, she claimed, was benign. Her followers were to be atheists, but she denied any dreams of closing churches or synagogues. Yet she missed no opportunity to put in a good word for atheism or to show the damage theism does the human spirit. It was in fact her enthusiasm for atheism that led her to make the infamous Mike Wallace interview statement that the cross is a symbol of torture, that it teaches men to sacrifice superiority to inferiority,[23] a statement she would live to regret—and to deny.

Her denials led only to further misunderstandings. The fact was that Objectivism demanded atheism, and religion was the enemy. In the *Playboy* interview she told Alvin Toffler that she never called the cross a symbol of torture, nor did she say she preferred the dollar sign, the symbol of free trade and thus of the free mind, to it. This was all "cheap nonsense." But she went on to say that she did consider the dollar sign the symbol of free trade and a free mind; and she admitted that she regarded the cross as "the symbol of the sacrifice of the ideal to the non-ideal." It seemed to her that "Christ died on the cross not for his own sins but for the sins of the non-ideal people"; and since in the name of that act men are asked to sacrifice themselves for their inferiors, "that is torture."[24] The lines of distinction are ever so dim and thin.

Any embarrassment this incident caused her did not keep Rand from further criticisms of the church. In 1967 she condemned Pope Paul VI's *Populorum Progressio,* charging that it demonstrated Catholicism's "impassioned hatred for capitalism." She seemed delighted that mysticism had shown its true colors. Mysticism, she went on, is antilife, for it hates to see men free and happy on earth, productive, climbing to the stars. She said that in recent times, as proved by this encyclical, the church had abandoned the great Thomas Aquinas and stepped backward toward the mind-hating, life-hating Augustine. It was marching toward a new dark age. The pope's words here were a "Requiem for Man" (*C,* 297–315).

As we have seen, Rand's major complaint against American conservatism was its ties with religion. Leaders like William F. Buckley sold a "package deal" of capitalism and mysticism. Since mysticism's altruism and capitalism's self-interest are mutually exclusive, this "deal" is both logically contradictory and ideologically confusing. For Rand the best argument for capitalism is that it gives men self-esteem, while mysticism gives only oppressive humility. She longed to see a new breed of dedicated radical capitalists rise from the ashes of America's mixed economy, men and women free of all traces of theism (*C,* 194–201).

Feminism

Rand was one of only a handful of successful American female novelists of the twentieth century. She was one of an even smaller group of successful female philosophers. By achieving both distinctions she was perhaps unique. It is therefore interesting to analyze her attitude, as a successful woman, toward womankind. Here, as in other dimensions of her thought, Rand was unconventional, unpredictable, provocative, and radical.

It is a generally accepted notion that men do not create convincing female characters for their fiction. With the possible exceptions of Somerset Maugham and Tennessee Williams, male writers seem able to portray only men. Rand successfully created male characters, preferred them, it would seem, often giving her women secondary roles; but her women, who had leads in the early works and near leads in the major ones, are as remarkable and memorable as any in fiction. Whether they are as convincing as they are remarkable depends perhaps upon whether one accepts Rand's sense of life. In either case they are memorable.

The women of the early fiction include the sad Irene Wilmer of "The Husband I Bought," the vivacious, zany Jinx Winford of "Good Copy," the wistful Claire Nash of "Her Second Career," and the courageous Frances Volkontez of "Red Pawn." With Frances there is a distinct change of direction, attitude, and personality from the earlier women, perhaps because Frances is born of Rand's soul. She is neither tragic, cute, nor unfortunate. She accepts her lot, follows reason, and faces consequences with head held high. With her Rand begins to fashion women of enormous physical and psychological strength and beauty, feminine in appearance but masculine (by the definition of Rand's day) in temperament, will, and performance. Their only weakness is their weakness for men.

Karen Andre of *Night of January 16th* defies convention and public opinion to serve the needs of Bjorn Faulkner. Kira Argounova of *We the Living* sleeps with two men, the second to save the first, but ends her life alone and without apology, trying to escape the land that has made her what she is. The simple Gaea of *Anthem* is something of a reversion to earlier days, a woman of less will and intelligence than Karen and Kira; yet she too has the mind, will, and courage to flee her totalitarian state, and she succeeds where Kira failed. Like Kira and Karen, she wants nothing so much as to kneel at the feet of a great man.

In Dominique Francon of *The Fountainhead* Rand created a woman of great intellect and individualism who marries two wrong men because the love she shares with the great, right man Howard Roark is too good for a marriage bed in this imperfect world. Dominique is, by her creator's own admission, Ayn Rand in a bad mood. But Dagny Taggart of *Atlas Shrugged* is the woman Rand had sought all her life, herself in a good mood, at her best. Dagny is bright, rational, independent, productive, and sexually both promiscuous and selective. She dominates every scene without being obnoxious and makes love to her heroes without lowering herself to the level of mistress, wife, or mother. She shares the spotlight in Rand's circle of stars only with Karen Andre and Kira Argounova; and of the three she is the brightest and best.

It is easy to see, through the pages of her novels and plays, what Rand thought—consciously, unconsciously—of the feminine character. Implicitly evident in her fiction and explicitly stated in her philosophy is the conviction that women stand in awe of the superior male. "I am a man-worshipper," she told Edwin Newman. She said she wanted to look up to men, for to her this was an important part of being feminine. Women who do not accept the natural superiority of men, she said, are not really feminine.

Rand said that women can do any type of work, that no job is forbidden them, but that no true woman would want to be the boss of a man. She could not vote for a woman for president because a woman is not psychologically equipped to rule men. The essence of femininity is hero worship.[25] Even her Kira, Karen, and Dagny bask in the reflected glory of their man. Barbara Grizzuti Harrison has noted that Rand's are strong, dominant women subdued by stronger, more dominant men who stoop to kiss their ankles before raping them. They are perfectly capable of running the world but prefer to serve as playthings for males of the species.[26] They are content, despite their will and intelligence, to say to men, as does Gaea to Prometheus in *Anthem:* "Your will be done" (*A,* 105).

There is also in Rand's fiction, never acknowledged by its author or admitted by her followers, a *Tosca* theme. Her women all tend toward multiple love affairs, often more than one at the time, always of course for a noble purpose. Frances Volkontez of "Red Pawn" and Kira Argounova of *We the Living* make love to one man, in both cases a communist official, in order to save another, in both cases an enemy of the communist state. Dominique Francon of *The Fountainhead* makes love to Howard Roark but marries two other men before finally marrying him, just to prove her perverse point that their love is too good for this world. Dagny Taggart of *Atlas Shrugged* makes love to at least three of the book's heroes and seems poised at story's end to make love to all three and maybe to all four—all for the noblest of purposes. All three, or four, are like-minded rational capitalists, her kind of man because she is their kind of woman. Perhaps somewhere in Rand's psyche lay a desire for more than one man at a time; and while her philosophic essays never mention the fact, she probably believed her own wish was rooted in universal femininity.

Even more obvious in her fiction and even less admitted outside it, more obvious than the desire for multiple love affairs, is Rand's conviction that for a woman lovemaking is best when it is violent. At least three of her heroines are gloriously raped: Karen Andre the first time she meets Bjorn Faulkner in his office; Dominique Francon the first time she is alone with Howard Roark and virtually every time they meet thereafter; and Dagny Taggart when at last she meets the elusive John Galt in a New York City train tunnel. Sex is best, Dominique explains in her story, when the rapist holds his victim in utter contempt; and she refuses for years to marry Roark because she prefers extramarital rape to conjugal lovemaking. She considers husband Peter Keating's sincere passion for her absurd and will not make love to Gail Wynand on their cruise because it is what conventional people would expect her to do. Sex for Rand and her women should be a selfish act, performed by a man who wields his penis as roughly as he wields a stone drill in a quarry. There are strong hints of sadism and masochism in the pages that had to pass rather strict censors in the 1940s and 1950s. They speak eloquently if mysteriously of the personal perversions of Rand's heroines and by implication of women everywhere.

Rand of course said plainly that love is a fulfillment of one's self, an expression of self-esteem. The object of one's love is important only to the degree that he or she fulfills one's own personal need. "Love is not self-sacrifice," she told Toffler in the *Playboy* interview, "but the most profound assertion of your own needs and values. It is for your own happiness that you need the person you love."[27] Only a man or woman with personal self-esteem, one who puts productive work above all else and self above the other person, can truly love. Only after Dominique has helped Roark blow up his housing project does she have the self-esteem to be his mate. Only then does she understand what Roark told her long before: "To say 'I love you' one must first know how to say the 'I' " (*F*, 400). Furthermore, like-minded men and women of rational self-interest immediately recognize each other when they meet, knowing they can share Rand's selfish love.

In Rand's stories men love other men without homosexual implications, for the mutual rational self-interest they share; and women recognize the men worthy to receive their worship the same way. As Francisco d'Anconia tells Hank Rearden in *Atlas Shrugged*, the person one chooses as a lover is his own mirror image. People of reason find and recognize and love each other (*AS*, 490). Yet Rand denied advocating promiscuity or hedonism. Pleasure, she corrected those who suggested such things, is a by-product and not a goal of love. "Only the pleasure which proceeds from a rational value judgment can be regarded as moral."[28] In real life her followers were not encouraged to act the way her fictional characters did. As a writer Rand was free, but as a woman she was conservative. Or so she said.

Despite her contention that "what is proper for a man is proper for a woman," presumably in sex as in labor, and despite saying that "women can choose their work according to their own purpose and premises in the same manner as men do,"[29] the feminist movement that sprang up after her 1964 *Playboy* interview caught her off-guard. She could not see what all the fuss was about. American women had things better than women anywhere on earth. They were loaded with luxuries and had a free choice of careers. She herself had held her own in a man's world and had succeeded as a playwright, novelist, and philosopher. The way she saw it, the women leading the feminist movement had to be man haters, out to start a sex war more violent than a class or race war. There would be a masculine reaction and rightly so. Women should first take jobs open to them, prove themselves, then climb the ladder. They should not seek subsidies.[30] Yet she said there should never be a woman president because women are psychologically unequipped to preside over men.

Philosophy and Fiction

Even as a young writer Rand had a clear picture of what she wanted to say and how to say it. There were of course many elements of her "sense of life" that took time to mature, many that she never recognized, many she would not admit. But in the second part of her writing career she reflected at length on her fiction and interpreted as best she could its meanings and implications. This is a rare thing for a creative writer to do, something that only one who turns from fiction to philosophy can do. It is also tricky, for there is no objectivity, and the musings must be accepted with a healthy skepticism. But it is interesting to see what the old Rand thought the young Rand had been trying to do.

"One cannot write about life without discussing philosophy," Rand often said. All novelists are philosophers because their fiction inevitably reflects their interpretation of human existence. Some are aware of their "sense of life" and some are not; some express it explicitly and some do not. She identified herself as one vividly aware and unapologetically explicit. Some borrow a "sense of life" either from other writers or from the prevailing philosophy of the day, while others create one of their own, out of personal convictions, often at odds with prevailing trends. She created her own and boasted of it (*FN,* preface).

The characters that populate Rand's fiction are born of her sense of life: heroes without flaws, villains without redeeming virtues; some more nineteenth century than twentieth, some more twenty-first. They are not the kind of people one meets on the street, yet they are more than symbols of nonmaterial ideas. Rand explained that she observed life around her, analyzed the way men act and why they do so, drew abstractions and captured the essence of motivation and moral virtue and vice, and then created characters from the abstractions and action from the motivation. Each of her characters is then an abstraction, each designed to demonstrate virtue or vice, all together telling a moral story.

Rand was undisturbed by the criticism that her characters do not appear in real life. She proudly admitted that while they had recognizable physical features they were abstractions, either all good or bad, each following his particular sense of life, each personifying a moral truth. Each character represented a sense of life for readers to study. Each one was a symbol of good or evil dressed in the real-life clothing of the work-a-day world.[31]

Romanticism

Rand called herself a romantic realist. By *realist* she meant that she wrote of this world and of present-day problems. By *romantic* she meant that she clearly delineated the choices in life that men can and should make, not just the ones they generally do make. She was critical of the naturalism she saw in most contemporary fiction because it dealt only in the choice men of the common order make in life, usually conformist and without authenticity. It dealt with the accidents, not the essence of life. She believed that she alone presented life as it ought to be, through the lives of men and women who make the choices they can and should make. She was not out merely to describe the world but to change it as well. Her heroes and heroines, men and women of rational self-interest, choose their own destinies amid the real choices of life.

Rand strongly identified with nineteenth-century romanticism, particularly with its earliest manifestations. She mourned its demise and riduled the naturalism that supplanted it. She said romanticism's greatness lay in its recognition of man's faculty of free choice; and she believed that she alone among modern writers retained this romantic sensibility. But she also recognized romanticism's fatal error, its glorification of rusticity and consequently its condemnation of industry. She called romanticism a brilliant adolescent that invented an ingenious philosophy of man, only to choke on its own excesses, follow a false trail, fail to create a single convincing hero, and fall by the wayside to be replaced by the dreary naturalism that prevails today. She saw it as her own mission, that of a writer born out of time, to keep the romantic tradition alive, to avoid the pitfalls that destroyed it, and finally to restore choice to its rightful place in human thought and action.

Rand believed that literature—and indeed all forms of art— should be judged by the image of man it projects. If the hero of a novel is strong, competent, productive, able through free choice and rational self-interest to find happiness in this world, that work is good. If not, it is not.[32] She denied that literature should teach lessons, but she said that it should certainly show men the way to a better life. It is, she once said, "the indispensable medium for the communication of a moral ideal" (R, 121–22). In Atlas Shrugged the composer Richard Halley explains to Dagny Taggart that an artist (here a musician) is a businessman, trading his wares for Understanding (AS, 78). Rand considered Victor Hugo the father of great fiction and Mickey Spillane one of his few true disciples, both because they present a clear choice between good and evil, both because they project a positive image of man.

Rand found most contemporary literature "philosophically immoral. Aesthetically, it bores me to death."[33] It had degenerated into the sewer and was devoted to depravity. She found it exhilarating that she was so often the object of denunciations, for it proved to her that she was the only modern novelist to declare openly that her soul was not a sewer, nor were those of her characters, nor were those of mankind. She believed that she was the only bridge between the promise of romanticism in the past and the hope of romanticism in the future. If there should be a romantic movement in days to come, she would be its morning star (R, v–vi).

Hope

The future often did not look bright to Ayn Rand. Public schools, stripped of their mission by "progressive" theories of education, failed to teach children to think conceptually. Universities, themselves devoid of ideological foundations, were responsible for America's loss of direction. Yet despite her pessimism she claimed she had hope for the future.

Americans, she said, were still capable of rejecting irrationalism and altruism. They could still repeal the welfare state and return to capitalism (*P*, 213–14). New intellectuals, inspired by Objectivism, could reestablish brotherhood with capitalist businessmen and march on to the victory the old intellectuals forfeited. Thus her battlecry, as she brushed away the dark clouds: "The intellectuals are dead—long live the intellectuals!" (*FN*, 67).

Chapter Five
Ayn Rand's Defenders and Accusers

In personal appearance Ayn Rand was not particularly attractive or provocative. She affected the cape and cigarette holder of Dominique Francon and Dagny Taggart, but her dark complexion and stocky build did not approximate the tall, ash-blond features of her heroines. One might wonder if a Howard Roark or a John Galt would have found the author as desirable as they found the women she created.

But when she opened her mouth to speak or lifted her pen to write—and all her writing was done with pen and ink—this small lady with the dark, wide, bright eyes and the ash-blond voice became a tigress. She was more committed to her cause and more articulate in defending it than Dominique or Dagny ever dared hope to be. Only Kira Argounova and Karen Andre of her women came close to her passion and power. After she spoke, Roark and Galt would have been at her feet. Despite her physical appearance, her lack of dazzling beauty, she was extremely provocative. She was purposely, constantly argumentative. She demanded that every reader and listener take sides either for or against her. She looked, in Barbara Branden's words, always outward, never inward. She was always, completely right.

This is why she acquired such an array of disciples and detractors. No one could view her objectively or moderately. Those who read and reviewed her became ardent admirers or sworn enemies. There are perhaps more of the former still around than of the latter, but during her lifetime the latter predominated—at least in print. The thousands who joined her ranks, the millions who bought her books, are less represented in critical materials than those who reviewed her either for money or for the chance to argue with her. If accurate tallies could be made, it is likely her readers would divide about evenly, pro and con, and that most would feel passionately about her, with few standing on middle ground.

Romantics

First the defenders. Many defend their discipleship by saying that Rand was the truest, most uncompromising romantic writer of her day. They say they were attracted to her by the strength and resolution of her heroes and heroines, those men and women motivated and directed by rational self-interest. They like the clear eyes and smoke-filled hair and absolute certainty of egoists like Howard Roark and Dagny Taggart. It may have been a task at first to adjust to seeing such figures in modern rather than the usual medieval settings, as titans of industry rather than knights on horseback, as mistresses rather than damsels, but once they came to recognize her characters as modern guardians of romance, they delighted in her certainty and adventure.

These fans never go deeper than the story line. They read Rand's novels but not her philosophy. They likely never hear of her atheism—the most difficult of her teachings for romantics to accept—or even of her political, economic, or social radicalism. They are merely disgusted by the literature of the 1940s and on, literature featuring characters without conviction or purpose. They instinctively agree with Rand that literature should entertain and inspire. At times she might go a bit too far in making her point about self-interest; but she more than compensates by making her characters stick to their guns when times get rough and by rewarding them in the end with success and happiness.

Rand gives romantic readers exactly what they want: a temporary escape from the real world of cloudy moral decisions, laws made to protect the majority from exploitation by superior minorities, nine-to-five existence that offers no opportunity for heroism. Rand often railed against critics who called romance escapist, but it certainly is, and she was herself mistress of the escape artist's craft. Her fans read her precisely for this reason, for her ability to bring escapist nineteenth-century romance to our day.

More than this, she was not one of the large body of contemporary women romance writers who still tell of fair maidens saved from barbarians by white knights on horseback or of school mistresses who fall in love with widowed earls. This woman wrote "like a man," a man of the industrial age, yet one who believed in good and evil and the love born of the struggle between them. Her heroes invented new metals and ran corporations and erected tall buildings;

but they were still knights in shining armor. They were believable even when unrealistic, admirable even when arrogant, and both old and new enough to be intriguing.

Whatever one may think of Rand's fiction—its quality or philosophy—it is a great accomplishment. Those who like her writing, whether sophisticated or not, have defensible reasons for doing so. One such reason comes, surprisingly, from Nathaniel Branden some ten years after Rand purged him from the Objectivist movement in 1968. For some years after their separation he had pouted and ridiculed the woman he had worshiped, insisting that she had been like a father to him; but after the pain subsided, he was able to view her work more objectively. In a public address in 1978 he said that from early in her life her personality "crystallized in such a way that her destiny was to write *Atlas Shrugged.* In a very profound sense, that's what she came here for."[1] Its pages told the stories of heroes and heroines who followed rational self-interest to individualism and victory. She and her novel would live on through the achievements of young people inspired to gallant behavior, success in business, and personal fulfillment.

Capitalists

Perhaps second in popular appeal to her romanticism was Rand's defense of capitalism. The only label she ever wore was "a radical for capitalism," and she earned the right to wear it. She gave her readers the same right. Douglas Den Uhl and Douglas Rasmussen, who have published a comprehensive if a bit disjointed volume on Rand's philosophy, consider her the most successful thinker in modern times at merging a classical review of human nature with a nineteenth-century liberal interpretation of economics.[2] In a review of *Capitalism: The Unknown Ideal* for *Nation's Business,* Jeffrey St. John commended her as one of the few contemporary writers capable of presenting to young readers a rational defense of capitalism. She understood and argued with great dignity, he wrote, the morality of capitalism and the hope it offers the world. He suggested that businessmen endow chairs of economics in state universities to teach Rand's interpretation of American history and the capitalist ethic.[3]

Rand's interpretation and ethic were, as we have previously noted, unequivocal. Capitalism was for her the logical result of the Renaissance rediscovery of Aristotelian rationalism. It is the only economic system based on reason, the most practical, productive, moral system known to man. Those who practice it are the brightest, most ethical of men. Only the dull, the subversive, the mystical oppose it—and always in the name of the worthless masses. These sentiments filled the speeches and conversations of her fictional characters and later the public addresses she delivered and the articles she published as a philosopher. It is little wonder that she appealed to a generation of affluent young people heretofore taught to feel ashamed of their wealth and to feel responsible for the less fortunate. It is little wonder that Objectivism reached its peak of popularity during the 1960s, at the height of liberal social thought and planning.

It is doubtful that Rand's followers, except for the few who read all that she wrote and tried to make consistent, logical sense of it, fully understood what it meant to be a Randian radical for capitalism. Few of them followed her much beyond the rhetoric and into the deeper waters of pure laissez-faire economics. Most probably cheered her speeches and essays and went right back to government subsidies and commissions and the security of the corporate life Rand so despised. They were fair-weather disciples, willing to buy a book and attend a lecture and cheer her dramatic defense of liberty and individualism but unwilling really to opt for freedom or individualism themselves. She was immensely popular on a superficial level, as are most immensely popular leaders, providing listeners and readers with brief, orgasmic feasts of nostalgia; but her "capitalist" fans would not have survived many Objectivist winters.

Logicians

Another group of readers who found Rand exciting and attractive—for quite different reasons than those that excited and attracted romantics and capitalists—were searching for a philosophy of cold, logical certainty. Even when her reasoning was faulty, Rand gave her readers the feeling that they marched in step with Aristotelian logic, that they were rationally superior to the lesser mortals who followed tradition, emotions, or faith. Objectivism gave its adherents comradeship with like-minded disciples of logic, a sense of infallibility that a philosophy absolutely sure of its premises and conclusions can give its disciples.

For this reason Rand attracted to her camp a number of disciples, men and women of varying levels of philosophic expertise, who shared a common need for assurance against the uncertainties of modern philosophy. One of these disciples was Paul Lepanto, whose *Return to Reason: An Introduction to Objectivism* is the best example of the kind of books we may expect from the Rand school of thought in years to come. Lepanto attempts to collect, organize, and systematize the scattered elements of Rand's thought. The result is a reasonable, logical, analytical statement of a philosophy that may or may not make good sense but sounds erudite, as if it can bear the weight of someone searching for logical certainty. If one cannot accept its basic assumptions, particularly the assumption of rational infallibility, it will seem nonsense. If one can accept them, it is a wonderful discovery. It faithfully reflects the style that made Rand so irresistible to so many followers.[4]

Philosophers who do not accept Rand's Objectivism feel that it is precisely in her logical reasoning that she is weakest. William F. O'Neill in his book *With Charity toward None: An Analysis of Ayn Rand's Philosophy* says that most of her conclusions are wrong simply because she argues from faulty assumptions and uses faulty reasoning. Moreover, when she is right—as she is about conformity, alienation, the fragility of contemporary philosophy—it is for all the wrong logical reasons. At least she does have the moral and intellectual courage, he says, to make her bold, sometimes surprisingly accurate statements in spite of the terrible weakness of her premises and logical formulae.[5]

Robert Hollinger, writing on Rand's epistemology for the book by Den Uhl and Rasmussen, commends her for pinpointing major weaknesses of the modern philosophic establishment. He believes, in fact, that her major contribution to philosophy may be that she exposed more fruitful trails for future philosophers to follow than those laid down by the establishment. But he too, like O'Neill, finds her philosophy's internal structure tragically weak. Ironically, he says, she failed because of faulty logic to develop a workable theory of knowledge, the very area of philosophy she considered most important, the one she considered her major contribution to the rise of the new intellectual.[6]

What both of these men are saying is that Rand was weakest where she thought she was strongest and strongest in the very intuition she despised as an enemy of reason. She seemed to have a nose for the truth, yet she insisted on following twisting rationalistic paths that not only were fruitless but drew attention away from her native brilliance. She was more a mystic than are most theologians, yet she despised and condemned mysticism. She praised reason, yet it led up blind alleys. She was from earliest times more a creative than a philosophic person. Those who found comfort in her cool calculations were in fact dancing more to the music of Dionysus than of Apollo.

They are not to be ridiculed. Anyone who follows a master teacher or charismatic leader is responding more to the convictions of the teacher than to objective demonstration of truth. Rand was herself "the truth" of Objectivism. Her fictional characters were "real" to her and her followers, her assumptions valid, her logic solid, her conclusions unquestionable—all because she said so. Her followers considered themselves disciples of logic, even if the leader and her teachings were illogical.

Worshipers

A word that is heard again and again as Rand's followers explain her attraction for them is *certainty*. Rand was sure of herself, of the truth of her claims, and of the righteousness of her cause. Albert Ellis, one of her most severe critics, from whom we shall hear later, believes that her appeal lay in the religious nature of her teachings and method. In his book *Is Objectivism a Religion?* he lists ten religious characteristics easily found in Objectivism. Briefly stated, they are: dogmatism, absolutism, tautological thinking, intolerance, deification of heroes, anti-empiricism, punitive correction, obsessiveness, mysticism, and ritualism.[7] If he is correct in his analysis, then one key to Rand's popularity was and is her ability to provide a substitute religion for people who had lost their own or wanted to be rid of it or simply wanted to fool themselves into believing that they could escape religion without having to do so at all.

This being the case, it becomes all the more interesting to analyze Rand's constant indictment of religion: its belief in God, its mysticism, its altruism. Objectivism was supposed to be the polar opposite of these things: it was atheistic, rational, selfish. Yet all the time it may well have been for Rand's Objectivists not so much an antireligion as a substitute for religion, a new religion. She was their guru, the infallible pontifex manimus. She and her followers quoted her fictional heroes as if they were prophets of holy scripture. She demanded strict intellectual conformity to the faith. She perpetrated periodic purges of the unfaithful. The purged blamed her for psychological damage greater than any mere philosopher would have been able to do. Those who remained faithful, her loyal disciples, considered themselves morally superior to common men and women.

Her elite followers were and are fanatics. An example is the reaction of her second heir-apparent, Leonard Peikoff, to a critical review of *For the New Intellectual* by Gore Vidal in a 1961 edition of *Esquire* magazine. Peikoff's reply, also printed in *Esquire* later that year, was sufficiently hot to singe Vidal's neatly trimmed hair. Vidal had relegated Rand to the netherlands of unreadable novelists and had caustically commented that she should know, as did any intelligent person, that the altruism she so violently condemned is absolutely necessary for human survival. Peikoff replied that Vidal's defense of altruism meant that Vidal viewed society as one "gigantic sacrificial furnace in which men behave like moral cannibals and fight over who should be the victim of the moment."

He chided Vidal for losing his race for Congress in 1960, saying that the good people of New York had understood the implications of his altruism all too well; and as to the "mysticism" he says Vidal pushes: "It can tell men that their minds are incapable of grasping the 'higher' truth for which they need revelations—and then it is theology; it can tell men that they have no minds and are mere puppets dancing on the strings of economic history—and then it is dialectical materialism; and it can declare that it is unnecessary to think or analyze and sufficient to distort and to recite bromides—and then it is Mr. Vidal's review."[8]

This is quite an attack merely to refute what any reader would recognize as a flabby critique of Rand's first book of philosophy. It is of course much more than a verbal display of outrage at an unfair review. Rand was for Peikoff and the Objectivists more than a philosopher. She was in fact their religious leader, the bringer of Truth, someone to be defended as one would a saint. Objectivism was and is a religion, demanding the absolute loyalty of its faithful and earning the anguished hostility of its banished apostates.

For Personal Reasons

While Rand kept a large following of people loyal to her, some intimately and some peripherally, she provoked an equally large body of critics. Some of these never met her, or if so only briefly, and were disturbed, offended, or scandalized by what she wrote or said from the lectern. Others were—and are—former disciples who fell from grace and were purged or else chose to leave the fold of their own volition. The bones they pick are mostly professional ones, but their accusations are quite personal. Rand demanded an unqualified yes or no from those who heard her message; and both the yeses and the nos tended to be emotional. For those who first said yes and then no, the Objectivist experience left deep wounds.

One of her first former disciples to go public with his "j'accuse" was Jerome Tuccille, whose book *It Usually Begins with Ayn Rand* appeared in 1971, three years after the apostasy of Nathaniel Branden. Inspired by the Branden schism, dedicated to "deviationists" over the world, the books deals with Tuccille's enchantment and disenchantment with Rand and Objectivism. He calls it a libertarian's odyssey.

Tuccille admits that he was attracted to Rand, as were so many of his generation of young radicals, because she seemed to offer a plausible substitute for the crumbling religious faiths of America in the late 1950s and early 1960s: Catholicism, Judaism, Waspism. Objectivism was certain of its righteousness, and deviation from its orthodoxy brought quick, severe punishment. Yet its conformist members were encouraged to feel that they were actually radical nonconformists. For a long time Tuccille felt at home in the Rand household.

At first he accepted Rand's repeated contention that she was the only rational alternative to the conformist, corporate, collectivist America of the Eisenhower-Kennedy era. She elevated egocentrism to the level of a respectable philosophic principle. She taught that rational self-interest is the only proper motivation for human behavior, the only basis for productivity; and this appealed to a young man trying desperately to free himself from the altruism of his upbringing. She condemned the welfare state, and this appealed to a young individualist. He naturally assumed that she stood for individual freedom of will as well as political freedom of choice.

What he discovered, to his embarrassment and then to his horror, was that the advocate of freedom and individualism was in truth a stern dogmatist who would not permit her followers to question her closed system. It became more and more evident to him that Objectivist discussion was little more than testimony in praise of

Ayn Rand, that the enforcement of orthodoxy brought slavery with
its security, that he admired deviationists more than the loyal elite
of the movement. The champion of individualism and of the un-
fettered mind had erected a collectivist prison, and her disciples
were the inmates, enslaved by their devotion to her. Reality was
what Ayn Rand said it was; morality was conformity to Ayn Rand's
ethic; and rationalism was thinking Ayn Rand's thoughts after her.[9]

Even the terminology Objectivists were required to use was defined by Rand's drive for conformity. Heroes were men who acted
like Howard Roark and John Galt; rationalists were people who
followed Rand's teachings in every detail; thugs, hoodlums, savages,
degenerates, weaklings, altruists, second-handers, looters, and mus-
cle mystics were those who questioned and disagreed with her. At
last, Tuccille says, he could no longer stomach the dogma: Mickey
Spillane and Ian Fleming are the heirs to Victor Hugo and the only
proponents of romanticism, other than Ayn Rand, in the modern
era; altruism is to blame for all the political and economic woes of
the twentieth century; a man and woman can find sexual bliss only
if they share an identical moral, ethical, and intellectual code—and
of course recognize each other immediately upon first meeting. As
to this last point, he guessed that Objectivists could so easily spot
each other in a crowd because they all tended to look like the
characters in Rand novels: tall and lean, with firm jaws and confident
eyes, thick wavy hair, and of course they all smoked cigarettes in
silver holders and wore gold brooches or tie pins shaped like dollar
signs.[10]

Tuccille dropped out of the movement in the late 1950s, as he
found Rand's behavior growing ever more bizarre; as one member
was read out of fellowship because his wife could not bring herself
to be an atheist; as another was denounced as "anti-life" because he
did not take up cigarettes; and finally as Rand became so entranced
by a cha-cha dance instructor that she required her followers all to
learn Latin rhythms, the "most rational" of music, the kind most
compatible with Objectivism.[11] Tuccille, like other former Objectivists, drifted on into Libertarian party politics; and at the time
he wrote his book he seemed still to be drifting, like so many other
former disciples of Ayn Rand.

A second person to register a personal, and even more anguished,
complaint against Rand for what discipleship did to him was Sid
Greenberg. His 1973 book *Ayn Rand and Alienation,* privately printed

with advertisements for his other books included, and rather care-
lessly edited, seems an obvious attempt to strike back at people
who had hurt him deeply. It is a humorous book, at the end rec-
ommending as an alternative to Randian ethics his own "Sidean"
formula. Yet it is also a book brimming with pain.

Greenberg acknowledges his intellectual debt to Rand and Branden for "certain concepts and theoretical formulations" that helped
him see the importance of acquiring "an integrated view of existence." But he quickly goes on to say that this debt was paid and
overpaid by the suffering he endured while a member of the Objectivist sect. If happiness can be considered a currency, he says,
then Rand and Branden owe "a moral debt" to everyone "emotionally
hampered" by the content and manner of expression of Objectivist
ethics. A short story included among his rambling chapters tells of
a young Rand disciple who goes out to practice Objectivism on a
construction job and is beaten senseless by his fellow workers who
do not immediately see the good sense of his philosophy. This is
undoubtedly a parable of Greenberg's own experience out in that
real world Rand never taught her followers was there.

Greenberg agrees with Tuccille that despite its rejection of religion Objectivism is in reality itself a religion. Being an Objectivist
was, he says, like being a member of a religious sect. Hand-picked
apostles like the Brandens acted as Rand's priests to the members
below them, to those less perfect than they, teaching them how to
grow in Randian grace. A catechism prepared by Leonard Peikoff
kept followers from philosophic deviation. Discussion sessions for
the inner circle featured repetitious testimonies to the wisdom of
Rand's thought. In public meetings, when Branden spoke and Rand
answered questions from the great unwashed, any comment that
did not agree with Objectivist orthodoxy was labeled irrational and
the person making it severely chastised. Deviationists and irration-
alists either shaped up or shipped out, while hopeful initiates waited
in trembling anticipation to be declared worthy of the name Objectivist. The result of all this, he says, was a band of emotional
cripples dependent upon "spiritual healers" for their secular
salvation. [12]

Greenberg makes a lot of the "Objectischism" that occurred when
Branden was purged from the inner circle of disciples. He describes
in some detail the shock and outrage as disciples learned in piecemeal
fashion that the Founder's heir-apparent was guilty of deception,

exploitation, and moral transgressions. There were even rumors that Branden was being banished because he had rejected Rand's sexual overtures. He says that those who wished to remain in the movement were required to take loyalty oaths to Rand and Objectivism. The Nathaniel Branden Institute was dissolved, Branden headed off into the California sunset, and those who lost faith drifted away into politics or into their own private worlds of philosophic inquiry. Greenberg became first a doubter and then a deviationist and finally an apostate. He later claimed that it saved his sanity.

After all his reflection on his experience with Rand and Objectivism, Greenberg concludes that the movement was doomed from the start by its premises. It held a false dichotomy between reason and emotion. For Rand any thought or deed that is not the result of rational consideration is immoral. Since Greenberg knows from experience that happiness results from a proper balance of reason and emotion, he believes that Objectivism cannot give happiness and makes those who do find it feel guilty. [13]

It is true that Rand emphasized reason and rejected emotion as a way of knowing the truth. It is also true that she believed only those ideas and actions born of rational analysis could be morally good. But she did believe that rational thought brings happiness, pleasure even, and that she never told her followers they must be gloomy. Yet almost every observer of Objectivism's public meetings noted the lack of humor and joy among its members. Greenberg may be right when he argues that Objectivism discouraged the kind of pleasure that perhaps comes only from irrational impulses, that encourages and provides unproductive recreation.

Perhaps the most significant critic of Rand's philosophy and its effect on personal life, his included, is Nathaniel Branden. Branden joined Rand as a disciple in 1950, when he was a twenty-one-year-old university student; and he was purged from the movement he had helped found and develop in 1968, when he was thirty-nine. Starting over in California at the age of forty, with a new wife, he opened his Biocentric Institute and proceeded to write books such as *The Psychology of Self-Esteem, Breaking Free, The Disowned Self, The Psychology of Romantic Love, The Romantic Love Question and Answer Book, If You Could Hear What I Cannot Say,* and *Honoring the Self.* It is in the latter that he speaks most candidly about his relationship with Ayn Rand.

He acknowledges that he stayed with her even after he had realized that their relationship (what it was he does not say) was detrimental to his well-being. He says that only after their separation did he realize fully why he had for so long jokingly called her his father: she had for many years filled his need for a strong, masculine image to imitate. He calls the separation in 1968 a painful experience for him, and he now disassociates himself from her psychology, but he still contends that her ethics will stand the test of time.[14]

Soon after he was purged Branden sent a defense of his actions to all *Objectivist* subscribers; and in due time he distributed a tape explaining the schism from his own perspective. But it was not until ten years later that he delivered, in a public address, his most thorough critique of Ayn Rand. It was at *Reason* magazine's tenth anniversary banquet that he spoke; and his remarks, while not extemporaneous, were in answer to the question why Rand was not present at this gathering of people dedicated to individualism and capitalism. Branden told the audience that while Rand was a unique genius who had made many positive contributions to American discourse, she was also a highly suspicious woman, preoccupied with the loyalty of her followers, and not only viewed herself as a martyr but created her own martyrdom.

He wondered if her peculiar behavior were the result of the "terrible intellectual loneliness or isolation of the starting years" when no one understood or appreciated what she said and of "having absorbed a great deal of hurt, or intellectual or personal rejection." Whatever the cause of her aberrant behavior, he said, "nothing is more common among innovators than increasing suspicion of the slightest deviations among followers." Rand exhibited such behavior more with each passing year.

It was totally unrealistic, Branden went on, to expect bright young followers like hers not to move forward in their thinking, away from her themes and theories; but expect it she did, and she would tolerate no deviation and thus no progress. "It can never be the case," he moaned, "that you are going to create a living intellectual system" that all your followers will find completely satisfying. What made Rand's expectations of loyal conformity all the more ridiculous was that she proclaimed herself the champion of independent thought.[15]

According to Branden, she became in time an unbearable school mistress. Anyone who rejected her ideas she considered a lunatic; but anyone who passed them on she accused of stealing her thought.

To write *Atlas Shrugged* was Rand's destiny, he admits, and "in a very real way, she died when she finished it." Yet he continued to serve her and help create the atmosphere that seems to have warped so many of her disciples, including himself. He acknowledged ten years after seeing her for the last time: "I really feel, when you add it up, that the luckiest beneficiaries of her work are the people who read her and never see her, never meet her, never have any reason to deal with her in person." Take her ideas and develop them, he said with real pain, but never expect anything of her as a person. "Don't expect help. Don't expect understanding. Don't expect sympathy. Don't even expect sanity. Say, 'Thank you,' and let go."[16] Yet that was something she had to force him to say and do.

For Philosophic Reasons

Few of Rand's readers knew her personally; and the less one knew her the less personally one took her flaws. Still a number of people who knew her only from afar have attacked her philosophic shortcomings with vigor. Robert Hollinger, in the study by Den Uhl and Rasmussen, criticized her roundly for failing to provide her followers with a workable epistemology. Simply saying "*A is A*" and "existence exists" does not prove that the human mind perceives reality; nor does it explain how reality can be perceived.[17] Since the first step for a philosopher to take in formulating a defensible philosophy of life, particularly one that people are expected to embrace as a faith, is to demonstrate that one knows what one is talking about, it would seem that Rand was a failure.

There are other critics who contend that, whether or not she successfully established a credible epistemology, her work contains enough false assumptions to render it invalid. William F. O'Neill argues in his book-length critique of Objectivism that no philosophy can rest securely on Rand's false dichotomy between faith and reason. To reason requires first a faith in the rational process, just as any intelligent faith demands rational verification. Rand's refusal to admit that there is actually no inherently logical reason for rational thought, no rational reason for trusting logic without a faith presumption of the validity of rationalism, renders her entire philosophic system indefensible.

She was equally wrong, O'Neill argues, to support the false assumption that faith is merely a blind acceptance of laws and principles that violate reason. Faith for the intelligent person, and one such person was the Thomas Aquinas whom Rand claimed as a mentor, is the acceptance of laws and principles that lie beyond the power of man's mind to prove or disprove.[18] O'Neill found Rand hovering in countless places cleaving her false dichotomies, broadcasting her false definitions, making herself an easy target for the enlightened, thoughtful student of philosophy.

J. Charles King, another of the contributors to the book by Den Uhl and Rasmussen, finds the greatest flaw in Rand's Objectivism her deadly assumption that the rational man or woman will inevitably, invariably choose a life of productive labor. In point of fact, King says, many rational persons, even those who take pleasure in productive labor, may choose to pursue capitalistic enterprise only part of their lives. Some may choose to spend a greater or lesser part of their time pursuing leisure activities. Some may choose to earn their money early and spend their later years pursuing hobbies or causes that are neither materially productive nor financially profitable. Some may choose to spend their whole lives in pursuit of dreams that Rand would consider frivolous.

Such men, when they delight in unprofitable or unproductive pleasures, are not hedonists; and such men, when they do community service, are not detestable altruistic collectivists. They merely have different "tastes" from men who pursue productive work without respite. Man's reason can lead different men to make different choices; and no choice is more rational than others.[19] It would seem that Rand once again tends to limit rather than expand the human spirit. What was reasonable to her should not be taken as the standard for all men. As a workaholic, she assumed that being a workaholic was rational; and perhaps it is, despite medical evidence to the contrary; but it should not be the only path men of reason are told to take.

Related to this bit of logical error is Rand's contention that a rational person will always choose a rational mate. In point of fact, as proved by simple observation, a rational person, depending on taste again, may choose a variety of mates. Rand's own mate was not her intellectual equal; yet Frank O'Connor had other gifts that were obviously more important to Rand than intellectual ones; and she remained his wife for fifty years. Again the Rand straitjacket proves ill-adapted to human life. The life of reason is far broader, richer, and more flexible than she knew or would admit.

Still other critics of Objectivism have taken aim not so much at Rand's assumptions and logic as at the results of her assumptions and logic. An example is the work of Christian evangelical John W. Robbins, who in his 1974 book *Answer to Ayn Rand* claimed to be the first person to accept a dare issued ten years earlier by Nathaniel Branden: "No one has dared publicly to name the essential ideas of *Atlas Shrugged* and to attempt to refute them." Boasting "With the publication of this book, that statement no longer stands," Robbins proceeds to argue against each of Rand's theories by showing what he considered their inevitable negative results.

Her metaphysics, he says, is best described as objective reality, and the logical consequence of such an assumption is indestructible matter, entirely unacceptable to a biblical literalist. Her epistemology is reason, and the logical consequence, when it rules out other ways of knowing, is skepticism, also unacceptable to an evangelical. At this point it would be easy to dismiss Robbins—as he would be dismissed summarily by Objectivists—as just another mystic preaching the virtues of irrationality; and many thinkers outside his religious persuasion doubtless would agree here with the Objectivists; but in the second pair of his four arguments he strikes a more universal chord of complaint against Rand.

Her ethics, he says, is self-interest, as she so proudly boasts; but the logical consequence is as often as not the very hedonism she detested. Her politics, so she says, is capitalism; but if one follows her line of reasoning to its ultimate conclusion, it becomes anarchy.[20] Rational self-interest may be a contradiction in terms: given the character of human nature, human reason may well fulfill itself by seeking pleasure, not productive work. Rational self-interest that results in production is always limited to a small elite, smaller than the one in Galt's Gulch. Rand's capitalist utopia would lead to anarchy because she offers no arbiter for disputes between competitors except a rather naive faith in the rationalism of capitalists.

Rand based her entire system of thought on the foundation stones of reason and realism, which she claimed Aristotle had set in place for future generations. She considered herself an expert on Aristotle's thought; and while she disagreed with him on certain points, she called herself an Aristotelian. Yet many of her critics charged her with misunderstanding and misinterpreting the very man she claimed as her philosophic mentor. Jack Wheeler, writing for the collection by Den Uhl and Rasmussen, admits that Rand's heroes possess Aristotle's characteristic *megalopsuchia,* or self-centeredness; but he argues that she read her Aristotle selectively—and that she seems to have misread much of what she did read. While she credits him with the inspiration for her ethics, for example, she seems woefully ignorant of his and contradicts him repeatedly. Her angry, bombastic rhetoric stands in stark contrast to his even-tempered, well-reasoned style, demonstrating none of the resemblance to the master a disciple is expected to exhibit.[21]

Perhaps even more telling is the criticism of William O'Neill, who argues that despite all her verbal enthusiasm for Aristotle she is actually more Platonist than Aristotelian. She believes that truth is discovered and not created by the mind of man, that it has an identity independent of human intelligence, while Aristotle believed it to be a combination of discovery and creation. For Plato and for Rand, "basic truth is innate and is not therefore relative to life-experience in any sense at all and can easily be utilized as a ready criterion for assessing any subsequent interpretation of reality."[22] While Rand is not the first person to assume a false philosophic identity, this casts a shadow over her certain claim to the infallibility of Objectivism.

As noted earlier, Rand blamed Immanuel Kant for the sad shape of modern philosophy. Kant turned back the clock by questioning human reason, basing his ethics on a mystical sense of duty, opening doors to all kinds of fraudulent successors who have neutralized the great achievements of the Renaissance and left modern man emaciated on a dry and barren plain. Yet some critics have charged that Rand either misunderstood Kant or deliberately misinterpreted him so as to have a straw man to attack as she drummed up support for Objectivism.

She was wrong, say some, to claim that his critique of reason supports a mystical epistemology. It is primarily a tool to help man avoid the philosophic abuses pure rationalism sometimes brings to the world of thought. His defense of altruistic duty, while perhaps excessive, can be a corrective to the kind of cold self-interest that creates societies in which the poor have no alternative to violent revolt. William O'Neill, among her critics, accuses her of beating a dead horse. Kant's intuitive altruism is no longer attacked or defended in serious philosophic circles. The utilitarian altruism of

John Stuart Mill, which Rand seldom mentioned, is the current
power in ethics. Kant has been out of vogue quite some time, and
Rand did not know it.[23]

For Religious Reasons

With all the harsh words Rand had for religion, her indictment
of all forms of altruism, her outspoken atheism, it is not surprising
that some of her most caustic critics are religious writers. These
men are often, ironically, in basic agreement with her defense of
capitalism and might have become adjunct members of the Objectivist movement had it not been militantly atheistic. James Collins,
reviewing *For the New Intellectual* for *America*, while not writing from
a religious perspective, was the first critic to note her persistent
atheism. He considered it a fallacy to assume that since all the
people she hated believed in God all sensible people must be atheists.[24]
Joel Rosenbloom, reviewing the same book for the *New Republic*,
was the first to predict how her atheism would affect her audience.
Although he considered it "largely pretentious nonsense," its greatest weakness was its blatant, offensive antireligious polemic, which
would alienate right-wingers, her natural following, both in fundamentalist Protestantism and in the Catholic right.[25] He was right.
For these groups, capitalism and religion went hand in hand; and
Rand could only drive them away as she tried to budge them from
this "package deal." But she was happy to lose natural allies to keep
philosophic purity.

Typical of the fundamentalist Protestant reaction to her all through
her career was a *Christianity Today* article by Steven Cory, written
just after she died in 1982. Cory carefully explained that Rand was
an enemy of the faith, warning readers not to be tempted by her
politics and economics into swallowing her atheism. She was a
problem for fundamentalists, Cory said, a threat to the faith, because
she was the oddest of birds, an atheist who believed in free enterprise.
If taken seriously, she would make good capitalist Christians ask
the dangerous question: Is it necessary to believe in God to be a
good orthodox conservative?[26] His answer was yes, Rand's no. For
the fundamentalist whose God is the Protector of Big Business, Ayn
Rand is big trouble.

William F. Buckley's *National Review*, which represents the Catholic right, also found Rand a problem. Stanton Evans, in a 1967 article entitled "The Gospel According to Ayn Rand," praised her for her eloquent anticollectivism but scorned her opposition to religion. He compared her both to Walter Rauschenbusch—the Baptist minister and theologian who believed that one cannot be both a Christian and a capitalist—and to Karl Marx—who believed Christian mysticism robbed men of their classical freedom. Evans charged Rand with limiting the very human freedom she defended by telling her readers they could not believe in both human dignity and godly humility. Rand said God limits man's freedom, while the Catholic right considered God the author of freedom. By condemning the Christian culture that has given man more freedom than ever before in human history, Evans said, Rand rode alongside the collectivist barbarian hordes she claimed to fight.[27]

In addition to her atheism, Rand disturbed religious critics by her rejection of sacrificial love. Moderate Christians reacted heatedly to her denunciations of altruism. For Bruce Cook, writing in *Catholic World,* the ugliest thing about Rand was "her complete lack of charity," her provocative odes to selfishness, which gained media attention and spread her anti-Christian message abroad. He admitted that she did know how to win attention and get her message across to the public, this despite plots "absurdly tendentious," characters little more than "wooden puppets," and diction totally lacking in grace. He pictured her sitting in her "dark corner, surrounded by her followers, as persistent as a plague of lichens," singing her songs of selfishness to a naive, receptive audience.[28]

Liberal Protestants also found fault with Rand, both for her defense of raw capitalism and for her rejection of the love ethic. Charles Frederick Schroder, in a review of *For the New Intellectual* for *Christian Century,* mused that Rand's popularity lay in her appeal to young executives needing encouragement to make the long climb up the financial ladder and to older people who needed an excuse for their failure in the system. He called her "new morality" of rational self-interest no more than discredited nineteenth-century rugged individualism in modern garb. While he believed that she was too intellectual to have much impact on the average American, he worried over the effect her ethic of selfishness might have on impressionable minds looking for an excuse to pursue naturally selfish inclinations. He found her altogether deficient in social responsibility and warned that the kind of pride she advocated usually degenerates into mere vanity. She failed to see that interdependence is as important to human progress as independence.[29]

Generally speaking, outside religious circles Rand's atheism and ethic of selfishness brought more humor than alarm. *Newsweek,* in its review of *For the New Intellectual,* compared Rand to Aimee McPherson, calling her an evangelist for atheism and suggesting that she might prove false her assumption that America is suffering from altruism by taking a ride on a New York City subway.[30] Danger is of course in the eye of the beholder, and the religious press doubtless brought Rand more attention and influence by attempting to argue with her than if it had left her alone. She knew the reaction she would provoke with her atheism and ethic of self-ishness and almost certainly expressed them in terms she knew would get the attention and raise the hackles of God-fearing Americans.

William O'Neill, speaking as a Christian but with a more so-phisticated philosophic perspective than others, also found fault with Rand for her insistence that egoism and altruism cannot coexist. He expressed his disagreement with a rational distinction that chal-lenged Rand's claim to rational certainty. Her contention that one cannot live for oneself and also serve others he called patently absurd; and her descriptions of altruists as beggars, thieves, looters, and second-handers he called ridiculous. The rational mind, he said, can choose to fulfill itself through altruism, to derive self-satisfaction by granting a part of itself to others, if it so wishes. Contrary to Rand's assumption, altruism neither invites nor welcomes self-sac-rifice or suffering because it finds fulfillment in eliminating the sufferings of other men.[31]

As noted above, *Newsweek* compared Rand to a female evangelist, calling her a "she-messiah."[32] Many of her critics considered her the founder of a religion. Nora Sayre referred to her in the *New Statesman* as the "abbess of the acute right,"[33] and John Kobler in the *Saturday Evening Post* called her the Joan of Arc of a cult whose Cross of Lorraine is the dollar sign.[34] His use of the term *cult* to describe the Objectivist movement was quick to catch on and has been used many times. Bruce Cook, in a *Catholic World* article, called Objectivism a religion of high finance and Rand a missionary of uncommon zeal. He considered her and her message more de-structive of civilization than the Norse paganism of Paul Joseph Goebbels. She was a new John the Baptist, howling for One to

Come, a rational hero who would lead the world back to a producer's paradise.[35]

These brief references to Rand's evangelistic fervor and Objectivism's cultic power show that more than one hit-and-run observer found her more a theologian than a philosopher. Fortunately one observer went beyond catchy phrases to explain in detail the religious nature of Rand and her movement. Albert Ellis, a psychotherapist who once debated Nathanial Branden and was hooted down by an Objectivist crowd, wrote a book in order to say what he had not been permitted to say, even briefly, that night.

His book, *Is Objectivism a Religion?*, tries to show "that any resemblance between Objectivism and a truly rational approach to human nature is purely coincidental; that objectivist teachings are unrealistic, dogmatic, and religious; that unless they are greatly modified in their tone and content they are likely to create more harm than good for the believer in this way of life; and that they result in a system of psychotherapy that is insufficient and unhelpful."[36] Strong words. Ellis believes that Rand's teachings and the movement they inspired are a form of religion, one that is harmful to believers; and he wants to expose the business to the light of critical scrutiny. One finds it hard to disagree with Ellis's conclusions about Objectivism.

He shows rather conclusively that this movement dedicated to the death of religion is itself a religious movement. Its tone is dogmatic and absolutist, intolerant of disagreement with its basic assumptions. Its doctrines are definitional and tautological. It labels independent thought deviationism. It deifies its heroes, creating secular saints. It closes its eyes to empirical evidence that contradicts its assumptions and conclusions. It makes its adherents obsessive and compulsive. It is mystical, putting its faith in reason. And it follows strict rituals built around the person and thought of Ayn Rand.[37] It is not so much a liberator from as a substitute for religion. This is why it was condemned by established religious groups: it was their rival, and they knew it.

For Political Reasons

The political press was as loud in its criticism of Rand as was the religious. Her politics earned her as many enemies as friends. Honor Tracy, reviewing *Capitalism: The Unknown Ideal* for the *New*

Republic, demonstrated the emotion Rand could provoke. In her review, called "Here We Go Gathering Nuts," she took issue with the elitism issuing from Rand's praise of industrial-strength heroes and other accumulators of wealth. Rand hated the masses for being common and had no confidence in what she considered the ignorant majority. In a style more suited to Hyde Park's Speakers' Corner of the 1930s than enlightened political debate of the 1960s, Tracy concluded, Rand longed for a world safe for plutocracy.[38]

Rand's praise for rugged individualism, her encouragement of raw capitalism, her advocacy of rational self-interest were all anathema to the political left, particularly in the 1960s when it believed liberalism would soon come of age. Some members of the left relegated her to the dustbin of history, while others went to some lengths to rebut her. Both groups recognized that she was not a mainstream conservative. She called for less government than conservatives or even libertarians could imagine. She refused to compromise on even the smallest issue. Her movement, while small in numbers, was so fanatically devoted to her and her philosophy that should it ever turn political it could have a profound impact on American society. She was potentially the voice of a minority which, so long as it was led by conservatives, was benign but which awakened might threaten democratic majority rule because of its wealth.

The left feared Rand, but so did the right. Having over the years accepted certain features of collectivism, having tied capitalism to religion, the right found her also offensive and threatening. She was more severely criticized and her books more uncharitably reviewed in conservative than in liberal journals. William F. Buckley's *National Review* took issue with her with such heat that Rand once said that if Buckley walked into a room she would walk out. This feud began when Whittaker Chambers's review of *Atlas Shrugged,* entitled "Big Sister Is Watching You," appeared late in 1957.

Chambers called *Atlas Shrugged* "a remarkably silly book" and sniped that to call it a novel was to diminsh the genre. He was appalled by its dogmas, which he said were without appeal, and at its shrillness, which he said was without reprieve. He said Rand's mind was like a tornado, whipping up noise and dust, rejoicing in its power to demolish structures. He was offended by the pleasure she evidently took in portraying an imminent class war and by her gift for caricature, for painting every character in total black or white. She loved labels and effigies but hated real people with their mixtures of weakness and strength, their combinations and per-mutations of good and evil. She was particularly brutal to those not defined as heroic, the "looters" she lumped together into one "un-differentiated damnation."

Chambers judged that Rand owed much of her philosophy to Nietzsche, although she did not acknowledge it, and the rest to Marx. Both she and Marx, following in Nietzsche's footsteps, longed to clear away all religious cobwebs from the mind of man. "Randian Man, like Marxian Man," Chambers wrote, "is made the center of a godless world." Like Nietzsche she looked for a Superman to ride in on horseback and defeat the bureaucrats of mixed economies; and her Superman would inevitably become a Marxian Big Brother watching over every detail of human affairs. Rand's solution to the sad state of contemporary society would produce a far more potent strain of collectivism than the one she hoped to end. Her solution would be a fascist paradise. "From almost any page of *Atlas Shrugged*," he concluded, "a voice can be heard, from painful necessity, com-manding: 'To a gas chamber—go!' "[39]

Given such reviews and critiques, it is not surprising that Rand came to hate the self-righteous right. To be told that she was the willing if unwitting intellectual dupe of collectivism was a shock. To read Chambers's summation, that *Atlas Shrugged* was a patent medicine to be sipped cautiously, one that could do no lasting harm but might induce nausea, was to be insulted—and to conclude that the enemy included conservatives along with liberals. She recognized that she was persona non grata everywhere, that she could trust no one, and that she must save the world alone.

For Simplistic Thought

Then there are the critics who found fault with Rand and her thought not purely on personal, philosophic, religious, or political grounds but because she reduced her arguments to terms so sim-plistic as to misrepresent reality. At her death the *Times* of London described her vision as "a drastically simplistic interpretation of Romanticism which elevated and glorified man's self-determination at the expense of all other qualities." This led to "grotesque parodies of human characters and distorted human psychology" to such a degree that they were to the sophisticated reader unrecognizable.[40] The *Times* was not alone in this assessment.

Yet many of her readers loved her simplistic parodies and distortions; and Rand admitted she saw things in stark blacks and whites, calling gray a sign of uncertain commitment and compromise with evil. Bruce Cook once judged that her "writing seems totally free of any realization of the terrifying complexity of the individual soul and the world in which it exists."[41] Barbara Grizzuti Harrison called her fictional villains "straw figures" to be knocked down with ease by her verbal blows and allowed that she thought in a hermetically sealed world.[42] Gore Vidal noted that "she has a great attraction for simple people who are puzzled by organized society, who object to paying taxes, who dislike the 'welfare' state, who feel guilt at the thought of the suffering of others but who would like to harden their hearts."[43] But such criticism, if she even read it, did not change Ayn Rand.

Her simplicity was born of a conscious effort to draw bold distinctions between good and evil, to inspire her followers to pursue only the good, to allow no confusion that might impair judgment. It was also born of her refusal ever to change her mind or modify her theories or grow intellectually. In a postscript to *Atlas Shrugged* she wrote: "I have held the same philosophy I now hold, for as far back as I can remember. I have learned a great deal through the years and expanded my knowledge of details, of specific issues, of definitions, of applications—and I intend to continue expanding it—but I have never had to change any of my fundamentals." Assumptions that go unexamined through a lifetime harden to form a philosophy that is both intolerant and simplistic.

Men are either individualists or collectivists, she said as a young woman and continued to say, simplistically, as she grew older. They follow either their reason or some mystical directive, and only the ones who follow reason find the truth. They are either men of rational self-interest or detestable altruists, all good or all bad, never a mixture of the two. Religion is bad, capitalism good; big government is bad, small government good. Philosophers must see and speak in blacks and whites or they compromise the truth. Truth is truth, simply, absolutely.

Wallace Matson, writing for the Den Uhl and Rasmussen collection, noted how closed Rand was to even the mildest criticism and accused her of a "computer model of reasoning" that defined thinking as merely adding and subtracting facts to and from a set of prearranged concepts. She had, he said, rejected the more human and more honest model of thinking that permits new data to modify and synthesize with the old. He guessed that she stopped reading philosophy around 1945, just after the success of *The Fountainhead,* perhaps earlier, certainly by the time she began writing *Atlas Shrugged,* long before she began her career as a public philosopher. He noted that during the 1950s, 1960s, and 1970s, she fought opponents long dead, failing to acknowledge writers who were her contemporary rivals and even those who might well have proved her allies, separating herself purposely from the mainstream, rejecting those with related interests and concerns unless they openly espoused Objectivism.[44] Her simplicity was of course by design, and so was its corollary isolation. Ayn Rand was, because she wanted to be, *sui generis.*

Nathaniel Branden once said that a leader who sees his or her disciples changing can respond in one of three ways: by permitting reasonable ideological diversity, by separating on amicable terms, or by saying, "You're disloyal traitors, and I curse you." Rand always did the latter.[45] She believed that she had the truth, the whole truth, and nothing but the truth. She had known it since childhood, it had not changed, and she would not permit herself or any of her followers to tamper with it. It could be further illumined but not modified or improved. Her followers could explain but not reinterpret it. The prophet had spoken, the canon was closed, and there would be no further revelation. The gospel was simplicity itself.

The Future

Despite all the work of her critics, Ayn Rand remains a popular writer and philosopher. William O'Neill says she will continue to be read, at least on college campuses, for as far into the future as we can now see. She is, in his word, "doomed" to academic immortality. She has all the earmarks of a subdivision of a chapter in every textbook on American literature and philosophy to be written and of a half period in every lecture class on American literature and philosophy to be offered—well into the next century.

Her ideas, he explains, are simple and easily comprehended. She is extreme enough to be memorable and dogmatic enough to be easily classified. There is really no one like her either in American literature or American philosophy, making her a novel addition to texts and lectures that survey American thought. And not least she makes a nice, easy straw figure for teachers to demonstrate their argumentative skills.[46] A sad fate, this, for a woman who so loved to decapitate straw figures herself.

As time passes, as Ayn Rand the person subsides into oblivion, Ayn Rand the writer will not fade. Whether or not in the way O'Neill predicts, she will survive, flourish, and be sustained both by those who agree and by those who disagree with her philosophy. Both her fans and her critics, her defenders and her accusers, will rise up and call her blessed, for different reasons of course but with the same effect. It may not be the fate she would have chosen, but it is the fate she deserves.

Postscript: The Writer

It may be true that Ayn Rand will be remembered by professors out to make a point at her expense. It is almost certainly true that she will be remembered, in a wide circle, for a long time.

She will be remembered as a woman who invaded that last virtually exclusively masculine domain of academe, the field of philosophy. She will be remembered as the novelist who was not satisified to let her fiction speak for itself and who spent a quarter century explaining it. She will be remembered as the unsystematic philosopher who flaunted her lack of formal credentials, who purposely avoided the mainstream, who chose to challenge rather than try to make the team. She will be remembered as an odd, radical, uncompromising figure, as bizarre as the fictional characters she created. To be a woman philosopher who refused to conform to any established school of thought, who commanded more disciples than any writer of her day, who insisted on nonconformity in an age of conformity, these are the things that made her unique and will make her immortal.

She will also be remembered for her heroes, those unrealistic, unrealizable fictional characters her readers either scorn or love with such devotion. She will be ridiculed for oversimplifying character, for making "our guys" freedom fighters and "their guys" terrorists, for her weakness for "the rugged individualist" who asks nothing from and gives nothing to his fellow man, who is motivated by rational self-interest, and who always wins in the end. Others will conclude that her characters, as simplistic and exaggerated as they are, served as necessary correctives to the antiheroes featured in most of twentieth-century fiction.

She will be remembered as this century's chief defender of the human ego. Some writers can be reduced to a principle, some to a phrase, but Rand can be reduced to the one word *ego*. Some will ridicule her overemphasis on the self and explain it away by reference to Rand's feelings of inadequacy as a woman in a man's world, a Russian in America, and call it overcompensation. Some will have mixed feelings about it, as did historian Jacob Burckhardt when he discussed the ego: "The ego is at once man's sign of Cain and his crown of glory." Some will consider Rand a modern Montaigne, who wrote: "If the world finds fault with me for speaking too much of myself, I find fault with the world for not even thinking of itself." Some will consider her America's twentieth-century Walt Whitman, who said: "The whole theory of the universe is directed to one single individual—namely to You."

She will be remembered for her call to reason and her rejection of emotion, intuition, and mysticism. Some will chide her for giving no credit to what Dag Hammarskjold called "the steady radiance, renewed daily, of a wonder, the source of which is beyond reason." Some will dismiss her with the thought of Loren Eisley that the person who is not charmed by Circe's magic, who is untempted by the fragrance of Lotus, will end up a dry bone on the shore where Sirens sing of rational wisdom. Others will say that she spoke eloquently and with good cause for the rational nature of man against urges that call him back to the nature he must escape. Circe, Lotus-eaters, and Sirens tempt him away from his only source of truth, his reason, which alone can lead him through treacherous waters to his home.

She will be remembered as this century's most outspoken critic of religious mysticism and altruism. Some will accuse her of aiding and abetting the likes of Karl Marx, who called religion an opiate, although Rand considered it an opiate not so much for the masses as for the elite. Some will find fault with her for making humanitarianism and self-interest enemies. Others will argue that she simply tried to strip man of the convenient crutch that people unwilling to face the responsibilities and opportunities of life make of religion.

She will be remembered for her dynamic, uncompromising defense of capitalism, for arguing that when it is given a chance to work it brings peace, progress, and prosperity for all. Some will call her ignorant, and some will say she typified the bourgeois mind seeking relief from guilt. Others will admire her courage in defending a system that could in time prove the best of several imperfect economic choices. Still others will find her a necessary antidote to collectivism, agreeing with her that men lusting after money are less dangerous than those lusting after power.

She will be remembered for her unique interpretation of history, which identified the golden age as that nineteenth-century utopia when capitalism brought prosperity, racial harmony, educational advancement, and peace to the world. Some will dismiss her for her own dismissal of proletarian poverty, racial violence, educational failure, wars encouraged by newspapers fighting in capitalist competition. Some will find her heroic Vanderbilts villains and her villainous Roosevelts heroes. Some will perhaps find her odd revision of history a provocation to reassessment, a springboard to new perspectives and interpretations.

She will be remembered for her more than libertarian politics, for her refusal to endorse political parties, for her contempt for both liberals and conservatives, for her lack of interest in establishing an ongoing machine to achieve her goals. Some will find her impractical for advocating reform without supplying a working model to achieve it, while others will praise her for not building a new machine to dismantle the old one. Some will criticize her for cursing other libertarians, while others will praise her for challenging all "orthodox" political persuasions.

She will be remembered as the woman who established a secular cult. Some will recognize in her example the wisdom of Ignazio Silone: "I am saddened by all enterprises that set out to save the world. They are the surest way to lose one's self." Some will comment wryly that the woman who despised religion founded one of her own. Some will conclude that this was not only inevitable but necessary if Objectivist thought were to survive its creator. Whether Objectivism survives depends entirely upon the desire of future generations to believe, a religious impulse. Men think as they do because they believe as they do, and they believe what they will to believe.

Most of all, however, Ayn Rand will be remembered for her fiction, especially for *The Fountainhead* and *Atlas Shrugged*. These novels will be read long after her other books have been forgotten. She will be judged, as will Objectivism, by their quality. Some will dismiss them as they do all literature "with a message" to proclaim. Some will ridicule her trial scenes, her interminable speeches, her rapes, her preoccupation with erection. Some will either ignore or simply fail to notice the weaknesses as they thrill to the heroism, the romance, the happy endings. Some will be converted to Objectivism.

Ayn Rand's place in American literature and philosophy is yet to be determined. She awaits her destiny, and no one can predict it with certainty. However she is remembered, whatever value future generations place on her work, it is safe to say that the Russian immigrant girl who rose to national and international fame as a defender of what she considered American values, who lived her life as only her own unique sensibilities dictated, will indeed be remembered. For better or worse, there will never be another quite like her.

Notes and References

Chapter One

1. Nathaniel and Barbara Branden, *Who Is Ayn Rand?* (New York, 1962), 151–52.
2. "Disturber of the Peace," *Mademoiselle*, May 1962, 194.
3. Mimi Reisel Gladstein, *The Ayn Rand Companion* (Westport, Conn. 1984), 8.
4. Branden and Branden, *Who Is Ayn Rand?*, 158.
5. Ibid., 162.
6. Ibid., 165.
7. Gladstein, *Ayn Rand Companion*, 8.
8. Branden and Branden, *Who Is Ayn Rand?*, 173.
9. Ibid., 177.
10. Gladstein, *Ayn Rand Companion*, 9.
11. John Kobler, "Curious Cult of Ayn Rand," *Saturday Evening Post*, 11 November 1961, 98.
12. Gladstein, *Ayn Rand Companion*, 9.
13. Branden and Branden, *Who Is Ayn Rand?*, 180–81.
14. Ibid., 182.
15. Gladstein, *Ayn Rand Companion*, 9.
16. Branden and Branden, *Who Is Ayn Rand?*, 185.
17. Gladstein, *Ayn Rand Companion*, 11.
18. Branden and Branden, *Who Is Ayn Rand?*, 198–200.
19. Ibid., 204–5.
20. Gladstein, *Ayn Rand Companion*, 12.
21. Branden and Branden, *Who Is Ayn Rand?*, 224.
22. "A Steel House with a Suave Finish," *House and Garden*, August 1949, 35.
23. Dora Jane Hamblin, "The Cult of Angry Ayn Rand," *Life*, 7 April 1967, 98.
24. Paul S. Nathan, "Books into Film," *Publishers Weekly*, 11 June 1949, 2405.
25. Branden and Branden, *Who Is Ayn Rand?*, 224.
26. "Born Eccentric," *Newsweek*, 27 March 1961, 105.
27. Jerome Tuccille, *It Usually Begins with Ayn Rand: A Libertarian Odyssey* (New York, 1971), 21.
28. "Down with Altruism," *Time*, 29 February 1960, 94.
29. "Born Eccentric," 104–5.
30. Kobler, "Curious Cult of Ayn Rand," 98–101.

31. Alvin Toffler, "Ayn Rand: A Candid Interview with the Fountainhead of 'Objectivism,' " *Playboy,* March 1964; quoted from an *Objectivist* reprint, 3–4.

32. Hamblin, "The Cult of Angry Ayn Rand," 92–94.

33. Tuccille, *It Usually Begins with Ayn Rand,* 32.

34. Albert Ellis, *Is Objectivism a Religion?* (New York, 1968), 125.

35. Barbara Branden, *The Passion of Ayn Rand* (Garden City, N.Y., 1986), 257–343.

36. Nathaniel Branden, "Thank You Ayn Rand, and Goodbye," *Reason,* May 1978, 60–61.

37. Harriet Pilpel and Kenneth Norwick, "But You Can Do That," *Publishers Weekly,* 5 May 1969, 23–24. See also "Court Upholds Use of Name in Blurb," *Publishers Weekly,* 31 March 1969, 35.

38. "McGovern Is the First to Offer a Full-Fledged Statism to the American People," *Saturday Review,* 21 October 1972, 50.

39. Robert Hessen, "The Objectivist Periodicals," in *The American Conservative Press* (Westport, Conn., 1986), 12–13.

40. "The Chairman's Favorite Author," *Time,* 30 September 1974, 87.

41. Gladstein, *Ayn Rand Companion,* 17.

42. Barbara Branden, *The Passion of Ayn Rand,* 381.

43. Wolfgang Saxon, "Ayn Rand, *Fountainhead* Author, Dies," *New York Times,* 7 March 1982, 36.

Chapter Two

1. *The Early Ayn Rand,* ed. Leonard Peikoff (New York, 1984), 5; hereafter cited in the text as *E.*

2. *Night of January 16th* (New York, 1968), 3–5.

3. "Trial by Jury: Audience Dragged across Footlights to Act in Play," *Newsweek,* 28 September 1935, 29.

4. Greenville Vernon, "The Play," *Commonweal,* 27 September 1935, 528.

5. "New Plays in Manhattan," *Time,* 30 September 1935, 22.

6. Edith J. Isaacs, "Theatre Ballot Box," *Theatre Arts,* November 1935, 823.

7. *Night of January 16th,* 1.

8. *We the Living* (New York, 1959), ix; hereafter cited in the text as *W.*

9. *Anthem* (New York, 1946), v; hereafter cited in the text as *A.*

10. Rosamond Gilder, "Manhattan Music," *Theatre Arts,* April 1940, 236.

11. Philip T. Hartung, "The Stage and Screen," *Commonweal* 1 March 1940, 412.

12. Lorine Pruette, "Battle Against Evil," *New York Times Book Review,* 16 May 1943, 7, 18.

13. N. L. Rothman, "H. Roark, Architect," *Saturday Review,* 29 May 1943, 30–31.

14. *The Fountainhead* (New York, 1943), preface; hereafter cited in the text as *F*.

15. Nora Ephron, "A Strange Kind of Simplicity," *New York Times Book Review,* 5 May 1968, 8.

16. Roscoe Fristoe, "Patricia Neal: Able Actress," *Louisville Courier-Journal Magazine,* 21 July 1985, 11.

17. Patricia Donegan, "A Point of View," *Commonweal,* 8 November 1957, 155.

18. Richard McLaughlin, "The Lady Has a Message," *American Mercury,* January 1958, 144–46.

19. Granville Hicks, "A Parable of Buried Talents," *New York Times Book Review,* 13 October 1957, 4–5.

20. "The Solid-Gold Dollar Sign," *Time,* 14 October 1957, 129.

21. Whittaker Chambers, "Big Sister Is Watching You," *National Review,* 28 December 1957, 596.

22. Donald Malcolm, "The New Rand Atlas," *New Yorker,* 26 October 1957, 198.

23. Helen Beal Woodward, "Non-Stop Daydream," *Saturday Review,* 12 October 1957, 25.

24. "No Walls Will Fall," *Newsweek,* 14 October 1957, 131.

25. *Atlas Shrugged* (New York, 1957), 87–88; hereafter cited in the text as *AS*.

Chapter Three

1. "The Only Path to Tomorrow," *Reader's Digest,* January 1944, 88.

2. Ibid., 90.

3. "Note on a Bestseller," *Commonweal,* 3 January 1958, 349.

4. *For the New Intellectual* (New York, 1961), preface; hereafter cited in the text as *FN*.

5. *Philosophy: Who Needs It?* (New York, 1982), 58–70; hereafter cited in the text as *P*.

6. "Disturber of the Peace," 172–73, 194–95.

7. *The Virtue of Selfishness* (New York, 1964), vii–x; hereafter cited in the text as *V*.

8. Toffler, "A Candid Interview," 7.

9. "Goldwater People," *Look,* 3 November 1964, 53.

10. *Capitalism: The Unknown Ideal* (New York, 1966), vii; hereafter cited in the text as *C*.

11. *Introduction to Objectivist Epistemology* (New York, 1967), 1–4; hereafter cited in the text as *I*.

12. *The Romantic Manifesto* (New York, 1971), v; hereafter cited in the text as *R*.

13. *The New Left: The Anti-Industrial Revolution* (New York, 1971), 13–56; hereafter cited in the text as *N*.

14. "McGovern Is the First to Offer a Full-Fledged Statism to the American People," 50.

15. *Ayn Rand Letter,* 26 August 1974, 363.

16. *Philosophy: Who Needs It?,* 205–15.

Chapter Four

1. Toffler, "A Candid Interview," 5.

2. Ibid.

3. William O'Neill, *With Charity Toward None: An Analysis of Ayn Rand's Philosophy* (New York, 1971), 18.

4. "An Interview with Edwin Newman," tape from Palo Alto Book Service, made available in 1980.

5. "Note on a Bestseller," 349.

6. "Selfishness Without a Self," *Ayn Rand Letter,* 4 June 1973, 4.

7. *Night of January 16th,* 5.

8. Toffler, "A Candid Interview," 7.

9. "Disturber of the Peace," 194.

10. Donegan, "A Point of View," 156.

11. Toffler, "A Candid Interview," 9.

12. Tuccille, *With Charity Toward None,* 17.

13. Branden, "Thank You Ayn Rand, and Goodbye," 59.

14. "Disturber of the Peace," 172.

15. "An Interview with Edwin Newman."

16. "Tax-Credits for Education," *Ayn Rand Letter,* 13 March 1972, 1.

17. "The Only Path to Tomorrow," 88.

18. "An Untitled Letter: Part II," *Ayn Rand Letter,* 12 February 1973, 1.

19. "Philosophy: Who Needs It?" 53–54.

20. "Interview with Edwin Newman."

21. Toffler, "A Candid Interview," 12.

22. "Interview with Edwin Newman."

23. "Note on a Bestseller," 349.

24. Toffler, "A Candid Interview," 9–10.

25. O'Neill, *With Charity Toward None,* 24.

26. Barbara Grizutti Harrison, "Psyching Out Ayn Rand," *Ms.,* September 1978, 29–30.

27. Toffler, "A Candid Interview," 7.
28. Toffler, "A Candid Interview," 8.
29. Ibid., 7.
30. "Interview with Edwin Newman."
31. *Night of January 16th,* 1.
32. "Disturber of the Peace," 194.
33. Toffler, "A Candid Interview," 11.

Chapter Five

1. Branden, "Thank You Ayn Rand, and Goodbye," 61.
2. Douglas J. Den Uhl and Douglas B. Rasmussen, *The Philosophic Thought of Ayn Rand* (Urbana, 1984), 179.
3. Jeffry St. John, "Are American Students Flunking Capitalism?" *Nation's Business,* July 1967, 90.
4. Paul Lepanto, *Return to Reason: An Introduction to Objectivism* (New York; 1971).
5. O'Neill, *With Charity Toward None,* 13–15.
6. Robert Hollinger, "Ayn Rand's Epistemology in Historical Perspective," in *The Philosophic Thought of Ayn Rand,* ed. Den Uhl and Rasmussen, 56.
7. Ellis, *Is Objectivism a Religion?,* 175–77.
8. Leonard Peikoff, "Atlas Shrieked: Reply to Gore Vidal," *Esquire,* October 1961, 20.
9. Tuccille, *It Usually Begins with Ayn Rand,* 15–19.
10. Ibid., 23.
11. Ibid., 27–33.
12. Sidney Greenberg, *Ayn Rand and Alienation,* (San Francisco, 1977), 16.
13. Ibid., 21–25.
14. Nathaniel Branden, *Honoring the Self* (Los Angeles, 1984), 171–72.
15. Branden, "Thank You Ayn Rand, and Goodbye," 59–60.
16. Ibid., 61.
17. Hollinger, "Ayn Rand's Epistemology in Historical Perspective," in *The Philosophic Thought of Ayn Rand,* ed. Den Uhl and Rasmussen, 56.
18. O'Neill, *With Charity Toward None,* 100.
19. J. Charles King, "Life and the Theory of Value: the Randian Argument Reconsidered," in *The Philosophic Thought of Ayn Rand,* ed. Den Uhl and Rasmussen, 118.
20. John W. Robbins, *Answer to Ayn Rand: A Critique of the Philosophy of Objectivism* (Washington, D.C., 1974), 136.
21. Jack Wheeler, "Rand and Aristotle: A Comparison of Objectivist

and Aristotelian Ethics," in *The Philosophic Thought of Ayn Rand,* ed. Den Uhl and Rasmussen, 81–96.

22. O'Neill, *With Charity Toward None,* 85.

23. Ibid., 200.

24. James Collins, "Ayn Rand's Talent for Getting Headlines," *America,* 29 July 1961, 569.

25. Joel Rosenbloom, "The Ends and Means of Ayn Rand," *New Republic,* 24 April 1961, 29.

26. Steven Cory, "Rerouting Ayn Rand's 'Virtue of Selfishness,' " *Christianity Today,* 18 June 1982, 72.

27. M. Stanton Evans, "The Gospel According to Ayn Rand," *National Review,* 3 October 1967, 1060–63.

28. Bruce Cook, "Ayn Rand: A Voice in the Wilderness," *Catholic World,* May 1965, 119–24.

29. Charles Frederick Schroder, "Ayn Rand: Far-Right Prophetess," *Christian Century,* 13 December 1961, 1493–95.

30. "Born Eccentric," 105.

31. O'Neill, *With Charity toward None,* 201–2.

32. "Born Eccentric," 105.

33. Nora Sayre, "The Cult of Ayn Rand," *New Statesman,* 11 March 1966, 332.

34. Kobler, "Curious Cult of Ayn Rand," 98.

35. Cook, "Ayn Rand: A Voice in the Wilderness," 124.

36. Ellis, *Is Objectivism a Religion?,* 11.

37. Ibid., 173–77.

38. Honor Tracy, "Here We Go Gathering Nuts," *New Republic,* 10 December 1966, 27.

39. Chambers, "Big Sister Is Watching You," 594–96.

40. "Miss Ayn Rand," *Times,* (London), 8 March 1982, 10.

41. Cook, "Ayn Rand: A Voice in the Wilderness," 122.

42. Harrison, "Psyching Out Ayn Rand," 28.

43. Gore Vidal, "Comment," *Esquire,* July 1961, 26.

44. Wallace Matson, "Rand on Concepts," in *The Philosophic Thought of Ayn Rand,* ed. Den Uhl and Rasmussen, 35–36.

45. Branden, "Thank You Ayn Rand, and Goodbye," 60.

46. O'Neill, *With Charity toward None,* 24.

Selected Bibliography

PRIMARY SOURCES

1. Books

Anthem. New York: Cassell, 1938; New York: New American Library, 1979.

Atlas Shrugged. New York: Random House, 1957.

The Ayn Rand Letter. Palo Alto: Palo Alto Book Service, 1979.

Capitalism: The Unknown Ideal. New York: New American Library, 1966.

The Early Ayn Rand. Edited, with introduction, by Leonard Peikoff. New York: New American Library, 1984.

For the New Intellectual. New York: Random House, 1961.

The Fountainhead. New York: Bobbs-Merrill Co., 1943.

Introduction to Objectivist Epistemology. New York: New American Library, 1967.

The New Left: The Anti-Industrial Revolution. New York: New American Library, 1971.

Night of January 16th. New York: New American Library, 1968.

The Objectivist. Palo Alto: Palo Alto Book Service, 1982.

The Objectivist Newsletter. Palo Alto: Palo Alto Book Service, 1982.

Philosophy: Who Needs It? New York: Ayn Rand Library of New American Library, 1982.

The Romantic Manifesto. New York: New American Library, 1971.

The Virtue of Selfishness. New York: New American Library, 1964.

We the Living. New York: Macmillan, 1936; New York: New American Library, 1959.

2. Articles and Tapes

"An Interview with Raymond Newman." Palo Alto: Palo Alto Book Service, 1980. Tape.

"An Interview with Edwin Newman." Palo Alto: Palo Alto Book Service, 1980. Tape.

"McGovern Is the First to Offer a Full-Fledged Statism to the American People." *Saturday Review,* 21 October 1972, 50.

"The Only Path to Tomorrow." *Reader's Digest,* January 1944, 88–90.

SECONDARY SOURCES

1. Books

Branden, Nathaniel. *Honoring the Self.* Los Angeles: J. P. Tarcher, 1984. The latest of Branden's many books, it develops most fully his version of Objectivism as applied to psychotherapy. He speaks here of Ayn Rand's continuing influence on his life and thought.

Branden, Barbara. *The Passion of Ayn Rand.* Garden City, N.Y.: Doubleday, 1986. The provocative assessment of Rand's life and work by her most intimate female associate. Here one can find the fullest account of Rand's sexual relationship with Nathaniel Branden, told by one who shared the traumas of this odd love.

Branden, Nathaniel, and Branden, Barbara. *Who Is Ayn Rand?* New York: Random House, 1962. Nathaniel's résumé of Ayn Rand's philosophy is a bit obtuse; but Barbara's brief biography, while fawning, provides useful information.

Den Uhl, Douglas, and Rasmussen, Douglas. *The Philosophic Thought of Ayn Rand.* Urbana: University of Illinois Press, 1984. The authors define the parameters of Objectivism, calling on philosophers of varying viewpoints to analyze the various areas of interest and concern.

Ellis, Albert. *Is Objectivism a Religion?* New York: Lyle Stuart, 1968. This is a polemic against Objectivism by a psychologist who once debated Nathaniel Branden and who cogently if a bit dramatically argues that, despite her critique of religion, Rand created a new one.

Gladstein, Mimi Reisel. *The Ayn Rand Companion.* Westport, Conn.: Greenwood Press, 1984. The author provides an excellent, short biography of Rand before spending too much time surveying the major characters of her fiction and the major critics of her work.

Greenberg, Sidney. *Ayn Rand and Alienation.* San Francisco: Bridgeberg Press, 1977. This is a sad confession by a former Rand follower of the negative personal effects a deep devotion to her ideals can cause.

Lepanto, Paul. *Return to Reason: An Introduction to Objectivism.* New York: Exposition Press, 1971. A Rand disciple without critical pretentions, the author makes an admirable if unsuccessful attempt to systematize her thought.

O'Neill, William. *With Charity Toward None: An Analysis of Ayn Rand's Philosophy.* New York: Philosophical Library, 1971. This is an analytical, critical survey of Rand's thought, concluding that while she asked the right questions she most often gave the wrong answers.

Robbins, John W. *Answer to Ayn Rand: A Critique of the Philosophy of Objectivism.* Washington, D.C.: Mount Vernon Publishing Co., 1974.

Having stated his intention to describe and refute Rand's system of values, the author provides more description than refutation.

Tuccille, Jerome. *It Usually Begins with Ayn Rand: A Libertarian Odyssey.* New York: Stein & Day, 1971. This is another exposé by a disillusioned former disciple, painting a rather comic and at times frightening picture of the Objectivist Movement in action.

2. Articles and Tapes

"Born Eccentric," *Newsweek,* 27 March 1961, 104–5. An interesting description of an Objectivist lecture in New York, with Rand answering questions after a Nathaniel Branden address to the faithful.

Branden, Nathaniel. "Thank You Ayn Rand, and Goodbye." *Reason,* May 1978, 58–61. An explanation, ten years after the fact, of his break with Rand and his reflections on the influence of her personality and thought on his life.

"The Chairman's Favorite Author." *Time,* 30 September 1974, 87–88. An article linking President Gerald Ford's new chairman of the Council of Economic Advisers to Rand and Objectivism.

Cook, Bruce. "Ayn Rand: A Voice in the Wilderness." *Catholic World,* May 1965, 119–24. A rather uncharitable attack on Rand both for her poor writing style and for her denunciation of altruism.

Cory, Steven. "Rerouting Ayn Rand's 'Virtue of Selfishness.' " *Christianity Today,* 18 June 1982, 72. This article clearly demonstrates the problem fundamentalist Christians, despite their economic conservatism, had with Rand's atheism.

"Court Upholds Use of Name in Blurb." *Publishers Weekly,* 31 March 1969, 35. A discussion of Rand's suit against a publisher who used her name on a dust jacket without her permission.

"Disturber of the Peace." *Mademoiselle,* May 1962, 172–73, 194–95. The seventh in a series of articles on contemporary disturbers of conventional wisdom, centering on Rand's economic views.

"Down with Altruism." *Time,* 29 February 1960, 94–95. This covers a Rand lecture at Yale in which she spoke of the cross as a symbol of torture and condemned altruism.

Evans, M. Stanton. "The Gospel According to Ayn Rand." *National Review,* 3 October 1967, 1059–63. An attempt to place Rand and objectivism in the context of economic history and tradition.

Farnham, Marynia F. "The Pen and the Distaff." *Saturday Review,* 22 February 1947, 7, 29–30. Rand is included in a discussion of women authors and is recognized as a distinctly new breed.

Fristoe, Roscoe. "Patricia Neal: Able Actress." *Louisville Courier-Journal Magazine,* 21 July 1985, 6–12. Gives professional and fan reaction to Neal's performance in Rand's film *The Fountainhead.*

"Goldwater People." *Look,* 3 November 1964, 53. A discussion of the thought and motives of supporters of Barry Goldwater for president.

Hamlin, Dora Jane. "The Cult of Angry Ayn Rand." *Life,* 7 April 1967, 92–94ff. A brief description of the Objectivist lifestyle and a few comments on Rand's ethical values.

Harrison, Barbara Grizzuti. "Psyching Out Ayn Rand." *Ms.,* September 1978, 24, 26, 28–30, 34. One of the best brief analyses of Rand's personality, with a woman's view of her public philosophy.

Hessen, Robert. "*The Objectivist* Periodicals." In *The American Conservative Press.* Edited by Ronald Lora and William H. Langton. Westport, Conn.: Greenwood Press, 1986. A survey of Rand's periodicals and their place in the American conservative movement.

Kobler, John. "Curious Cult of Ayn Rand." *Saturday Evening Post,* 11 November 1961, 98–101. An analysis of the way Rand's personal experience influenced and reflected her thought.

McDowell, Edwin. "Ayn Rand: Novelist with a Message." *New York Times,* 9 March 1982, B6. A commentary on Rand's life and work at the time of her death.

"Miss Ayn Rand." *Times* (London), 8 March 1982, 10. An obituary.

Nathan, Paul S. "Books Into Film." *Publishers Weekly,* 11 June 1949, 2405. The story of the publicity buildup for the release of the film *The Fountainhead.*

Nichols, Lewis. "Talk with Ayn Rand." *New York Times Book Review,* 13 October 1957, 16. An interview with the author of *Atlas Shrugged.*

"Note on a Bestseller." *Commonweal,* 3 January 1958, 349. Contains verbatim selections of the printed copy of a television interview between Ayn Rand and Mike Wallace of C.B.S.

Peikoff, Leonard. "Atlas Shrieked." *Esquire,* October 1961, 14, 20. The official Objectivist reply to Gore Vidal's attack on Ayn Rand, which had been published in the July 1961 edition of the same magazine.

Pilpel, Harriet F., and Norwick, Kenneth P. "But You Can Do That." *Publishers Weekly,* 5 May 1969, 23–24. The story of the ultimate failure of Rand's suit to restrain a publisher from using her name without permission on a book dust jacket.

Rosenblatt, Roger. "The Rugged Individual Rides Again." *Time,* 15 October 1984, 116. A comment on the propensity of Americans to see themselves as the type heroes Rand describes in her novels.

Saxon, Wolfgang. "Ayn Rand, 'Fountainhead' Author, Dies." *New York Times,* 7 March 1982, 36. An evaluation of her work at the time of her death.

Sayre, Nora. "The Cult of Ayn Rand." *New Statesman,* 11 March 1966, 332. A discussion of Rand's place as "abbess of the acute right."

Schroder, Charles Frederick. "Ayn Rand: Far-Right Prophetess." *Christian Century,* 13 December 1961, 1493–95. A critique of Rand's thought by one who obviously hopes it will have little effect on American society.

"The Solid-Gold Dollar Sign." *Time,* 14 October 1957, 129–31. A caricature of Rand that shows her caricaturing mankind in her novels.

"A Steel House with a Suave Finish." *House and Garden,* August 1949, 54–57. A description of the San Fernando Valley home Rand occupied in the 1940s.

Toffler, Alvin. "Ayn Rand: A Candid Interview with the Fountainhead of 'Objectivism.' " *Playboy,* March 1964. (Text reprinted by *The Objectivist* in 16 pages used here.) The most comprehensive interview Rand ever gave, with opinions on issues ranging from capitalism to human sexuality.

Vidal, Gore. "Comment." *Esquire,* July 1961, 24, 26–27. Discusses the recent success of Rand's books but dismisses her as "an odd little woman," provoking Peikoff's reaction.

3. Reviews and Critiques

Chambers, Whittaker. "Big Sister Is Watching You." *National Review,* 28 December 1957, 594–96. Review of *Atlas Shrugged.*

Collins, James. "State of the Question: Ayn Rand's Talent for Getting Headlines." *America,* 29 July 1961, 569. Review of *For the New Intellectual.*

Donegan, Patricia. "A Point of View." *Commonweal,* 8 November 1957, 155–56. Review of *Atlas Shrugged.*

Ephron, Nora. "A Strange Kind of Simplicity." *New York Times Book Review,* 5 May 1968, 8, 42–43. Retrospective review of *The Fountainhead.*

Gilder, Rosamond. "Manhattan Music." *Theatre Arts,* April 1940, 236. Critique of *The Unconquered.*

Hartung, Philip T. "The Stage and Screen." *Commonweal,* 1 March 1940, 412. Critique of *The Unconquered.*

Hicks, Granville. "A Parable of Buried Talents." *New York Times Book Review,* 13 October 1957, 4–5. Review of *Atlas Shrugged.*

Isaacs, Edith J. "Theatre Ballot Box." *Theatre Arts,* November 1935, 823. Critique of *Night of January 16th.*

Letwin, William. "A Credo for the Ultras." *Reporter,* 11 October 1962, 56, 58, 61–62. Review of *Who Is Ayn Rand?*

McLaughlin, Richard. "The Lady Has a Message." *American Mercury,* January 1958, 144–46. Review of *Atlas Shrugged.*

Malcolm, Donald. "The New Rand Atlas." *New Yorker,* 26 October 1957, 194–98. Review of *Atlas Shrugged.*

"New Plays in Manhattan." *Time,* 30 September 1935, 22. Critique of *Night of January 16th.*

"No Walls Will Fall." *Newsweek,* 14 October 1957, 130–32. Review of *Atlas Shrugged.*

Pruette, Lorine. "Battle Against Evil." *New York Times Book Review,* 16 May 1943, 7, 18. Review of *The Fountainhead.*

Rosenbloom, Joel. *"The Ends and Means of Ayn Rand." New Republic,* 24 April 1961, 28–29. Review of *For the New Intellectual.*

Rothman, N. L. "H. Roark, Architect." *Saturday Review,* 29 May 1943, 30–31. Review of *The Fountainhead.*

St. John, Jeffry. "Are American Students Flunking Capitalism?" *Nation's Business,* July 1967, 90. Review of *Capitalism: The Unknown Ideal.*

Tracy, Honor. "Here We Go Gathering Nuts." *New Republic,* 10 December 1966, 27–28. Review of *Capitalism: The Unknown Ideal.*

"Trial by Jury: Audience Dragged Across Footlights to Act in Play." *Newsweek,* 28 September 1935, 29. Critique of *Night of January 16th.*

Vernon, Grenville. "The Play." *Commonweal,* 27 September 1935, 528. Critique of *Night of January 16th.*

Woodward, Helen Beal. "Non-Stop Daydream." *Saturday Review,* 12 October 1957, 25. Review of *Atlas Shrugged.*

Index

165

061491